DON'T SUCK

AT BUSINESS

How to build a formidable business with speed, strategy, and a healthy dose of sarcasm.

KARA LAWS

ISBN: 979-8-9895161-0-0

Book Cover Design and Formating by Elev8 Designs Co. | www.elev8designs.co

Illustrations by Cami Hales | www.halesyeahdesign.com

For more information about Kara Laws visit www.LaunchedAcademy.com

LAUNCHED

A GIFT FOR YOU!

Discover how LAUNCHED has helped business owners find the tools and resources they need to build successful businesses.

Access a bonus workshop on how to build a solid foundation for your business so you can reach your goals faster, make more money, and avoid expensive mistakes.

All FREE with this book. That is how grateful I am that you are reading it. :D

CLAIM YOUR GIFT NOW.

Scan the code or visit:
launchedacademy.com/book-bonuses

To all the women who want something more.

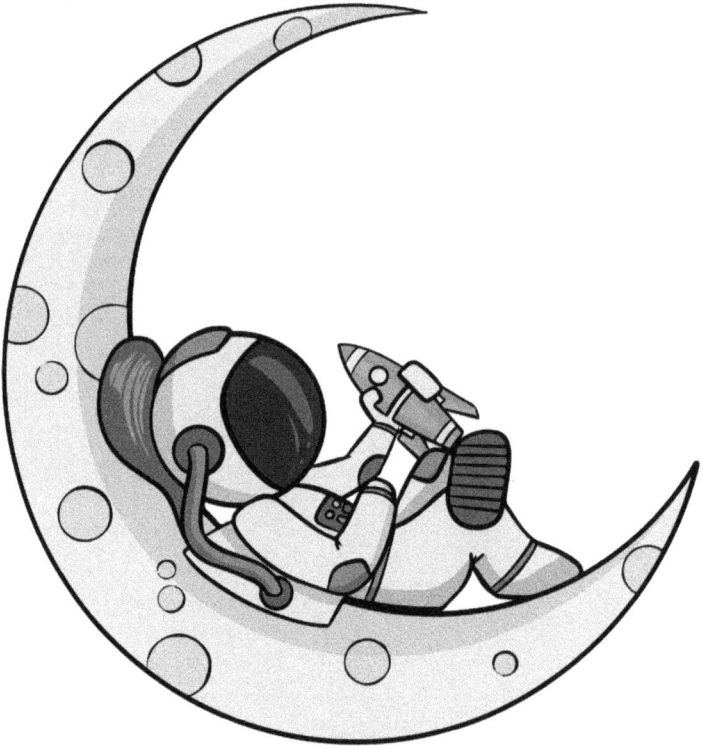

TABLE OF CONTENTS

PRAISE FOR LAUNCHED —————————————————— 8

PREFACE ———————————————————————— 13

SECTION ONE: YOU CAN DO HARD THINGS ———————— 19

CHAPTER 1: You Have a Product, Not a Business ———— 20

CHAPTER 2: Why Risk Business ————————————— 33

CHAPTER 3: Focus! Focus! Focus! ————————————— 52

SECTION TWO: GETTING STARTED ————————————— 73

CHAPTER 4: A Thriving Business Model ——————————— 74

CHAPTER 5: The Value of Powerful Branding ——————— 86

CHAPTER 6: Fans. Friends. Frustraters. Foes. ————————— 103

CHAPTER 7: Bringing Your Fans into Your Orbit ———— 120

CHAPTER 8: Why Can't I Find You? ————————————— 140

SECTION THREE: THE RACE TO PROFITABLE ——————— 161

CHAPTER 9: Finance That Finally Makes Sense ————— 162

CHAPTER 10: No Systems? No Business. ————————— 185

CHAPTER 11: Go Further Faster ————————————— 220

CHAPTER 12: Courage in Business ————————————— 234

WORKS CITED ———————————————————————— 257

PRAISE FOR KARA LAWS AND LAUNCHED

"At the first of the year, Kara and I had a great coaching session and definitely made a believer out of me regarding her knowledge and understanding of marketing via the internet, social media, etc. I had NO idea all of this was possible until our discussion. Kara knows what she is talking about, is passionate about what she is doing, and definitely enjoyable to work with. Our coaching session was one of the most enjoyable conversations I have ever had!

As a result, I updated my logo, made the necessary changes to my internet strategy, and have had my most successful year yet, in spite of the pandemic. Thanks Kara!"

- **Sydney Christensen**
Owner of The Red Geranium

"Kara was so helpful and easy to work with! I felt like I had a million questions and she answered every single one of them without making me feel dumb plus she always responded so quickly! I needed help adding a store checkout to my website and she came in and got it running super fast. Thank you!"

- **Amilia McKay**
Owner of Grapefruit & Thyme

"Phenomenal step-by-step information. The foundation of a business is critical and Launched will help you get started the right way. A plus, Kara's background in business gives this program personal grit. Two thumbs up!!"

- **Judy Howard**
Owner of A Best Clean

"I love love love that Kara is able to give me whatever step I need in the moment. This could be strategy, introducing me to someone, helping me make a decision, teaching me about process, explaining what's possible and many other solutions as the needs arise. Kara is kind and very patient with me as I learn how to manage and grow my businesses. She is creative and solution oriented. I credit her for the progress made in my business. I know I wouldn't have made this much progress on my own (I know this because I literally sat on the idea for 10+ years, ha!). Her knowledge and encouragement is so helpful to me. Kara is an amazing business coach!"

- **Christy Grant**
Owner of Event Derby and the Event Producer School

"Kara is so real, she is so kind, supportive and honest. She gives me real world feedback, works as my advocate and part of my support system. She gives me resources, makes introductions for me and really really cares about how myself and my business are doing. It has been a true pleasure getting to work with her."

- Tara Baker
Owner of Intimate Moab Weddings

"Kara is amazing. She is always able to pull me back on track when I start to make things difficult. She know that right questions to ask and pull extra stuff out of me. I always feel more clarity and confidence each we we talk. She has helped me get focused on each step I have needed to take. Kara is one of a kind. She always seems to know what I need next and is always encouraging, even when I am frustrated and maybe not following through with stuff I said I would then helps me start again."

- Gurgi Ruis
Owner of Purge Theory

"I have been really impressed with the business coaching Kara has offered us. We have a lot of ideas and also general direction that we want to go, but Kara has helped us break it down into actionable steps and also helped us know what order to tackle different tasks in order to make progress in starting our business. Also she has been very helpful in answering questions that would have taken us down a whole google wormhole to find the answer to and that has been really appreciated. I have been very happy with the services offered!"

- Loni Harris
Co-Owner of Spaghetti Tree Puzzles

"Kara's book is simply fantastic! It's dense, comprehensive, and yet still fun and easy to read! Her direct-but-honest and conversational way of explaining business principles is so refreshing. The entire time I was reading her book, I felt like I was enjoying a long afternoon with her on the couch getting all the deets I need to know about building a sustainable business. Whether you're struggling to get some traction in your business or you've just got a business idea and don't know where to start, this is the perfect manual to get you up and running the right way."

- Jennie Mustafa-Julock
Co-Owner of Jennie + Meredyth

"[Launched] is AMAZING!! Kara knows her stuff, and she's sincerely dedicated to supporting the small home town businesses she's involved with. Her professional services in marketing are top notch. She has been a tremendous influence in a successful rebranding for my small business."

- Lana Arthur
Owner of Patio Diner

"Such a detailed and informative session. Love how Kara explains and breaks down everything you need to know about having a successful business. Loved the pace of the program and how much information was shared. Things you can't get anywhere else."

- Sindho Channa
Owner of Career Coaching Sindo

"I love how she got so excited about my ideas! I always felt like I could talk things through with her and she would give me different perspectives and help me move forward! She was also so great about being willing to help me do research and find answers to my questions. I appreciated that she helped me set goals that would push me, and she was also very respectful of my time. Kara is the kind of person that you know truly cares about you in both your personal life about helping you be successful with your business! She boosted my confidence in my idea and more importantly in myself! She helped me learn how to set realistic goals, both short term and long term ones. As far as a specific goal, I designed a flyer for my product using a program she taught me how to use."

- Anne Marie Stapel
Co-Owner of Stapel Signs

"Kara is down to earth and real about business. I don't ever feel like she's "selling" me or pressuring me to do something that isn't in my best interest. She has so much experience with business and holds me accountable in just the right way. She has helped me to stay focused on building my business. I really like working with Kara. I reached out to her when I was feeling really lonely and desperate about my business and she has been a great support for me."

- Sharon Costanzo
Owner and podcast host of Keep Talking Revolution

"I wish I would have known about Launched and the Launch Your Business Academy before I started my business. I've now been in business for over a year and I'm still learning valuable lessons from Kara Laws will no doubt help me expand my reach and grow my sales."

- **Kimberly Flores**
Owner of FulFILLed Utah

"Launched offers simple, effective, straightforward solutions for solving new business challenges! Who do you know who is just starting out, who could use the gift of clarity, definitely check this out, it could be the perfect holiday present for a loved one, or maybe that loved one is you?!

Their work shops are fire for anyone just starting out in business, who really wants to start out right!"

- **Lauren Gale**
Owner of Lauren Gale Coach

"I attended a LAUNCHED workshop and it offered the most practical (and might I add fun), step-by-step business plan. This was really my first interaction with Kara, and she was so engaging that I hired her as a coach! She gave a step-by-step framework that I'm actually looking forward to going through and checking off the to-do lists. I would highly recommend the content she creates."

- **Brandy Wilkins**
Owner of Defining Point Coaching and Consulting

"I just started my business and the stars aligned to put Kara directly in my path. Cannot say enough good things! There are a lot of business coaches and educators out there, but few are as authentic, caring and approachable as Kara and her team. The courses are dripped out intentionally slow so you're forced to really take your time and not rush through building your foundation. It IS that important and she GETS that. The material is also super digestible and focused. Not a ton of filler. I'm not sure if this course was designed with the neurodivergent entrepreneur in mind, but the program is perfect for this auDHDer. Thank you SO MUCH for all the handholding and cheerleading! <3"

- **Christian Palmer**
Owner of Pogs and Jello Tarot

"Kara is a business genius. She has created Launched Academy to teach entrepreneurs and small business owners all her secrets to starting and maintaining a successful business. Having an experienced business owner, who has made and sold many companies, pass on her expertise is the key to starting on the right track. I 100% recommend Launched Academy to anyone willing to put in the work to get your business off the ground."

- Melissa Pupo
Owner of Get Seen Management

"This book combines the author's special brand of humor along with practical advice to help make your business a success."

- Cami Hales
Owner of Hales Yeah Design

"Your sarcastic wisdom and knowledge is the hard wake up and solution to my problem of feeling stuck, lost, and like an utter failure. Every word was written with tough love and genuine care. You have no idea how much I appreciated reading your book, and I am so excited to get home from vacation and start implementing and taking action! Thank you for writing this book and letting me beta read it. It gave me so much freaking clarity and direction."

- Rebekah Meredith
Owner of Rebekah MeredithCreative

🪐 PREFACE

"Starting a **BUSINESS** is different than selling some stuff."

Starting a real business requires so much more than having a product. The "so much more" is what this book is about.

You may have noticed *(or maybe you didn't)* that all the reviews above this preface are from names you probably don't recognize. I didn't spend time seeking out big names to write me a forward or give me a review or beta read my book for me.

My team and I talked about it. We talked about pulling all our connections to get us the highest and biggest names we could get. We even had some really cool people on our list.

In the end, we decided you wouldn't really care.

I didn't care.

When I was starting my first business I didn't care what millionaire and billionaire investors were endorsing. Maybe I should have. But in all honesty, I really wanted to know was, who could help someone like me.

I wanted to hear from people who were like me. I wanted to know how women were getting started, I wanted to know how to manage the chaos, I wanted to know where to find support. I wanted to know when the money started happening. Where was the money?!

So, my team and I decided to strategically feature reviews and feedback from people who were most like our readers or directly served our readers. We wanted you to hear from people who get you. You are not in this alone, and I wanted you to know that from the very start.

I digress, onto the rest of the book.

BUSINESS BOOKS ARE BORING AF

Seriously, Yawn.

I am an avid reader. Not finishing a book invites bad ju-ju. I am not about that.

And yet, I have never finished a business book.

Business books give me 70,000 things to do, they take forever to get to the point, and they are so boring! I would much, much rather re-read some weird sci-fi fantasy than admit I am a schmuck who falls asleep while reading.

WHY WRITE A BOOK

So, why am I writing a business book? Because this is the business book I needed but could never find.

This is the business book that would have easily saved me over $100,000.

Countless business owners find themselves in sticky situations. This is the business book hundreds of business owners asked me to write when they realized those sticky situations were *avoidable*.

There are humans all over the world who want profitable businesses but have no idea how to get there.

This book will give you the steps, easy steps, to getting your business launched and making real money.

STEP-BY-STEP. IN THE RIGHT ORDER.

Learning to run a business is frustrating. We Google our business questions and get twenty-five conflicting answers. Or we don't know what to Google at all. How do you Google, "Why is my business a ridiculous disaster?" and get helpful results?

What about, "What *don't* I know about my bookkeeping?"

My clients were exhausted *(and overwhelmed)* from combing through endless business advice for each new topic. They were terrified of making the wrong choices.

More importantly, my clients were sick and tired of making expensive mistakes that could have been avoided.

I have long lost track of how many times I have heard, "Where were you when I started? This information alone would have saved me over _____!" Sometimes that number is $500, sometimes it is a couple thousand, and sometimes is well over $40,000.

For me it was over $100,000.

This need is how the Launch Your Business Academy started. It is also why I am writing this book. I wrote this book so business owners all over the world can know how to manage and build their businesses correctly.

TO THE POINT

Let's jump in.

You are here because you are building a business and you have no freakin' idea how to get moving or what all the "rules" are.

I am here because I have helped hundreds and hundreds of business owners start and grow their businesses. I know some stuff, you don't know some stuff. I am here to share the stuff I know so you can know more stuff.

Teamwork.

(If you put your hand on the page we can pretend we just high fived. Seriously, do it. I did it! Did you? I really did it. Don't leave me hanging.)

THE SARCASTROPHE

Before we move forward in this book there is one thing you should know. Sarcasm oozes from my very soul. I don't know how to contain it, it just leaks out at the most inappropriate times. I once had a boyfriend break up with me because of my "smart alec attitude". I asked him what it felt like to be the boring one.

The odds of this book being filled with sarcasm is high. However, my sarcasm gets me in trouble in real life, when I think the joke is obvious. I can't imagine the trouble I will be in for sarcasm in writing, when you can't see or hear me.

In order to combat this lack of communication I would like to introduce you to the sarcastrophe. It is like quotation marks but for sarcasm. It looks like this, ^. When you see ^, you will need to read the next sentence in your largest sarcastic voice. ^Use those voices in your head.^

Get it?

ONWARD HO!

Let's move along.

I literally have nothing else to say here. I hate preamble. I hate small talk. I just want to get to work. My business coach is going to have a big lecture for me when she sees this. But you are building a business! You don't have time to waste while I fill pages to just fill pages.

Seriously, I just deleted 2,400 words for you. You are welcome.

Let's do this! On to actionable steps and education that doesn't make you want to curl up in front of the fire with a much more interesting book.

🪐 SECTION ONE
YOU CAN DO HARD THINGS

🪐 CHAPTER 1
YOU DON'T HAVE A BUSINESS

"Clearly these multi-millionaires were drunk."

When I was starting my first business, I binge-watched Shark Tank. It was on all of the time. I was obsessed. However, they just kept saying, "You don't have a business, you have a product." I didn't understand.

I thought a business WAS the goods it sold. If you are selling things then you have a business. ^Clearly these multi-millionaires were drunk. They definitely didn't have any idea what they were talking about. People with money.^

20

PRODUCT ≠ BUSINESS

As I write this I am more than fifteen years into business ownership. I have done all the things wrong and learned how to do a lot of things right. One of the things I did right? I finally learned the difference between a business and a product.

An entrepreneur that has a business, has a sustainable machine. It's predictable. There is a plan, a way to grow, a team to support it.

> A business is systems that work well, a brand that people can care about, and marketing that is actually profitable. A business is repeatable.

A product is none of those things.

Let me explain.

I was a professional wedding photographer for almost a decade. In the course of being a photographer you run across a lot of people who want to tell you how they took a good photo once too. ^Congrats^.

Because other people also, ^took a good photo once^, they often think they can do your job. Here's the difference between a professional photographer and my seven-year-old. A professional can do it again.

Anyone can take a photo. Anyone can take a great photo but a professional can produce the same results again, and again, and again. They can get those great photos in all situations. A professional photographer's great photos are not accidents. They are intentional.

That is what a real business is. It is not a successful accident. It is not a one-time viral video. It is not a hope and prayer and 10,000 photos with the hope one is good. A sustainable business is a business that can repeat and expand success over and over again.

A product is just a thing you hope people will buy.

A product is putting up a sign saying, "flowers" then waiting and hoping for people to show up. You have no plan, you don't know how to get the people to show up, you don't even know if you priced everything well. But you have flowers, and they are pretty so you hope people will come buy them.

A product is a hope and a dream. A business is the game plan.

FRANTIC OR FAMINE

I am a lover of systems and processes. If you can systematize it, you can repeat it. If you can repeat it, you can measure it. If you can measure it, you can adjust it and make it amazing. So, of course, I have a system for creating a successful business.

When I started my first official business I was twenty. I believed being good at my craft was all it would take to create a successful business. I was a very good photographer and fully anticipated that being good would make me wildly successful.

I just had to get out there, take some photos, show people what I could do and a raging success of a business would follow.

A raging success was not what happened. I had a product, not a business.

While I was good at getting in front of my audience and booking weddings, my business struggled. No matter how hard I worked, I was always in one of two camps. I was either fighting and scrounging to pay the bills or I was so buried in work I couldn't breathe.

I constantly felt pulled from all sides. Everything in my business was chaos.

I tracked everything from payments to whose photos were up next to each individual order in my head or in a notebook that seemed to always be lost.

I worked 12-18 hour days on the regular. I frequently forgot equipment, let clients miss payments, and was late on delivering photos. They looked great, but they were late.

At one point, I had this really amazing assistant named Anita *(name is not changed, she would like you to know she is amazing.)* Anita would show up at my house a few hours before every wedding, pack and double check gear while I frantically got myself ready in the background.

She created a checklist to keep us on track. Honestly, she was probably sick of panic driving back to my house to pick up the things we forgot. Her checklist outlined every single thing that needed to come with us for a wedding. She also created a "bride emergency kit". She wore it to every wedding. We were prepared for everything. And I do mean everything.

My clients loved us.

On the outside, I looked really put together. I had this amazing assistant, we were crazy prepared, we were fun to work with, and like I keep saying, we took great photos.

Behind the curtain, it was still chaos. The only thing together in my business was Anita.

This famine or frantic cycle continued for about five years. I lived with it because I thought that was what business ownership was supposed to be. Who was I to complain anyway? I was booking the weddings. I was getting published. I was having fun... when I wasn't crying.

But then I had my first kid. Damn, how those first kids ground us. He was such a sweet kid and the only child of mine that loved me more than his dad. His unplanned arrival in my life knocked my feet out from under me.

I still had weddings to shoot. I didn't have time to stop and have a baby, let alone take care of one. There was nothing in my business to support me through this. I was the business. There were no fallbacks, nobody to pick up the slack. It was just me. I had to keep going. I just kept pushing myself and pushing my body.

I was still shooting twelve plus hour weddings when I was eight and half months pregnant. I am fluffy so I hid it well. I didn't tell my clients I was pregnant. I didn't want anyone to think I couldn't do things. Pregnancy, however, made me really sick. I threw up in more than one wedding venue bathroom. My sweet husband was my second shooter by then and he politely covered for me while I tried not to vomit in bushes.

I didn't know how to have a business that supported me. I am not talking financially. I didn't have a business that actually supported me as a human being. My business didn't offer sick leave, give me time off, or even allow me a day's break. Having benefits like time off had never even occurred to me. Business was just endless work. I needed to be tougher.

And so I continued to push myself.

MY BODY BROKE

In the spring of 2015 my body couldn't take it anymore. My consistent, everyday feeling was stress. I was missing important family moments, from boating at the lake to my kid's second birthday. I was crying all the time. Every social interaction was a nightmare. I just felt lost.

Everyday I would ask myself, "Kara, what are you doing with your life?" I never knew the answer. I wasn't sleeping. I was stressed. Constantly stressed. I had had a lot of back issues for years leading up to the spring of 2015. Nothing helped. Then I woke up one morning unable to move.

I could hear my toddler crying in his bed, ready to start the day but I couldn't go to him. I could barely pull my broken body across the bed to reach my phone. I called my mom to come get my baby. How could I take care of a two-year-old when I couldn't even stand up? The pain was unbearable. Sitting

YOU DON'T HAVE A BUSINESS

was not an option, standing was not an option. I took all the pain pills I could crawl to then laid on my stomach on a padded bench. Not moving. Trying not to breathe.

AND STILL I WORKED.

I actually had a client who came over the same day to order cards for her daughter's graduation announcements. And I let her. I was high as a freaking kite on pain pills and still I worked.

Sometime after the back surgery I realized I couldn't keep living that way. I couldn't live a life where my family's income was dependent on me pushing my mental and physical health to the very edge. I couldn't live a life where I could never take a break. But,

> if I took a break, there wasn't enough money.

I had raised and raised my rates. I was the highest paid photographer in my entire county, some of the neighboring counties! But, it didn't seem to matter. I could never slow down because when I slowed down, the money stopped.

I felt trapped in my business.

🪐 BUSINESS OWNERSHIP IS NOT FOR THE WEAK

Business ownership is not for the weak or the casual. Most business owners push themselves like I pushed myself. Most business owners don't take vacations. They can't leave their business, they would lose income, too much income.

Most business owners are working themselves to their breaking points. Contrary to popular belief, most business owners are not drowning in money. In fact:

- 30% of small business owners don't take home any salary (Wood and Fundera)
- Less than 15% of business owners make $100,000 a year
- Only 9% of business owners make it to $1 million in revenue (A. and Small Biz Genius)
- Less than 2% of female business owners will participate in hitting that $1 million revenue mark (Zimmerman and Forbes)

The beginning stages of building a business are brutal. You have to figure everything out for yourself without getting paid for any of your work.

When you work a 9:00-5:00 you get paid even when you are just learning. When you own a business, no one is there to pay you to figure things out. You are your business. There is no management to teach you how to do things, no pre-vetted training to make sure you have all the knowledge.

You don't get paid to go to meetings, to network, to go to conferences, to participate in your local chamber of commerce. On the contrary, most business owners are being taken away from money making activities to attend these types of events.

Businesses are not created overnight. No matter how many video montages make it seem like business success happens overnight, that isn't how it works.

BIG DREAMS I COULDN'T REACH

I had big dreams for my photography studio. None of them involved me working 12-18 hour days. None of them involved me not being available to my family. Yet, that is where I ended up.

I didn't take any conscious steps to end up on that bench, breathing through my teeth as tears pooled underneath me. Complete debilitation wasn't a path I chose. It was a misstep, a mistake somewhere along the way and I had no idea where the mistake was.

Three years, another kid, and countless days of working stupid hours later, my mother talked me into going to a business retreat. The very first question they asked us was, "What are your fears? What about being here makes you nervous?"

With vulnerability that shocked me, I choked out, "I am afraid I have to close my business." Then I cried. I had spent the last three years trying to fix the problems in my business. I hired. I fired. I hired again. I raised my prices. I lost clients. I found trainings. I paid for business management help. I Googled and Googled and Googled. ^ No matter how many times I Googled, "Why isn't my business working?" Google never knew the answer. ^

I could not get out of the frantic or famine cycle. The business retreat was a last ditch effort to make my business work for me. This was it. If I couldn't find the solution at this retreat, it was the end of my business.

FIGURING IT OUT

At that business retreat, I learned about business. Not products, business. Not marketing, business. Up until that point, I didn't really understand business management. I did not understand the difference between a business and a product.

I didn't know what a business foundation was, or why it even mattered! I just kept running as fast as I could, hoping I would stop falling down.

This business retreat was the beginning of a whole new world for me. It was like a gear in my brain finally clunked into place. Everything I had been taught up until this point, and I took a lot of classes, were about the "flashy" parts of business. No one was willing to talk about the hard things.

No one was willing to talk about the boring things.

At this retreat I realized I had been running my business like a product. I was just going out and trying to sell that product one-to-one over and over again. I didn't have any systems. I made up my pricing. I didn't know why I charged over $6,000 for a wedding; someone who seemed smarter than me told me to raise my prices.

I didn't have any business strategy. I barely understood the basics of what a strategy meant.

I never had a foundation. I never had a stable business.

I had a product I called a business.

And it was eating me alive.

🪐 I TEACH BUSINESS BUILDING

I am very end-game. I don't like trends. I don't like fast cash scams. I like solid. I like sustainable.

> When a rocket LAUNCHES it isn't testing the waters. No one is giving that rocket half of their attention just to "see what happens". NO! When a rocket is launched it demands all of the attention.

Years of planning, building, and testing go into the launch of a rocket. It isn't a cardboard tube, it is a beautiful, well thought out, and intense process. The outside of the rocket has to be built correctly. The skin has to protect it from getting too hot. The nose has to be shaped correctly.

The payload has to be calculated and correctly accounted for. Different rockets are capable of carrying different types of cargo.

The guidance system needs to be correct and reliable. Rockets are not blasted into space without a path and a plan, nor should your business be thrust into operation without a clear path and plan.

When I talk about launching a business, I am not talking about hanging an open sign. Anyone can hang an open sign, just like anyone can take a photo. When I talk about launching your business, I am talking about LAUNCHING your business.

I am talking about creating the systems and direction to make sure your business accomplishes the mission you created it for. LAUNCHING a business isn't just having a product. LAUNCHING a business is creating the whole machine.

(And yes, I did spend a large amount of time learning about rockets just so I could make this comparison.)

A BUSINESS FOUNDATION

In order to LAUNCH a business that can reach your big goals, you need a solid business foundation. You have to understand business management, not just product pushing.

The business retreat I attended revealed my lack of a business foundation. I spent the next several years fixing my business, learning about business management, testing, and putting all of the pieces into a teachable system.

Business grows in very predictable phases. Most people understand that in order to start a business, you have to invest in the business. You have to spend money before you start making money.

There are places in your business when you will have to invest again. You will have to go down before you can go back up. This news comes as a shock to most business owners, who thought the investing was over. We call these s-curves.

The first major s-curve in your business will be your start-up phase. Here you will buy equipment, invest in some signage or maybe a website, you will purchase your product.

The second major s-curve is one most of us don't see coming. This s-curve, a place in your business when you have to re-invest in order to grow, happens when you cap out on personal time. This is when you need to hire people. It usually hits just under $100,000.

Most business owners find they really struggle to reach or grow past this $100,000 mark. Again, only 15% of business owners make it.

Creating a solid business foundation, and doing it right from the beginning, will help you cruise through this $100,000 s-curve. The more prep and understanding you have at the beginning of your business the less painful each s-curve is. You don't have to get stuck each time you reach for more, you can have the foundation to push through it.

WHAT IS YOUR MISSION?

> "We have stars in our eyes and a goal in our soul,
> nothing is going to stand in our way. Except ourselves."

It is really hard to know what you should be doing and what order you should be doing it in.

You have to go from place to place to place for all the different parts of your business. You have one woman who teaches marketing. Then you have to go somewhere else to learn about branding. But in the process you learned you should have started with branding and now none of your marketing makes sense and you need to re-make everything.

Or you have conflicting messages from everyone you go to. You learn about marketing from Suzy but then when you hire Johnny for website design he says Suzy is bat-face crazy. Then you hire someone else to teach you about copywriting and they say Johnny is drunk too!

As I fixed my own business then started and sold three others, I was recruited to start teaching business education. I was hired, through my consulting and education business, to start teaching other business owners how to fix their businesses.

I had about thirty clients a month that were sent to me through various entities. I very quickly learned I was not the only business owner who was stuck in the frantic or famine cycle. It was an epidemic. *Most* business owners were stuck; either frantically paddling to stay afloat or completely drowning from lack of cash.

By the time they got to me, they were in trouble.

It is funny how, as new business owners, we don't tend to like to get help. For me, it felt like it wasn't my win. If someone told me how to get there, I wouldn't get all of the credit. I didn't "do it on my own." ^ I want to go back in time to punch that girl. ^

She caused me so much heartache and stress that was never necessary, all because she was too proud to learn from others.

Many of us are like her at the beginning of our businesses. We have stars in our eyes and a goal in our soul, nothing is going to stand in our way. Except ourselves. Then we only reach out for help when we are in desperate trouble.

The business owners who came to me were usually in desperate trouble. They all had the same issue. They were pushing products instead of building businesses. They didn't understand business foundations. They had accidentally built the wrong life and they needed to know how to fix it.

9/10 times the fixes were costly. Re-building your foundation when you are 10, 15, 20 years into business is significantly harder and more costly than building it correctly from the beginning. I hated telling business owners they had to go backwards in order to go forward. I hate sitting on calls with them as they sobbed their hearts out because they screwed so much up at the beginning.

In an effort to help other businesses avoid these heart wrenching phone calls,

31

I partnered with one of the government entities I was working with to find the solution. We searched for the business program that taught new business owners all the steps, in the right order, at the beginning.

We searched for an affordable program.

We never found a good answer, so I created my own.

This book is a summary of that program.

If you are building a business, you don't have to build it alone. You don't have to make it all up as you go. You can have direction, support, and a community to help you reach your goals. You don't have to pay tens of thousands of dollars for help.

I put it all here.

NEXT STEPS

I actually didn't put it all in this book. I mean, I really, really tried but you would never read a book with all the business information. It would be 80,000 pages and you would fall asleep ^like a schmuck^.

So, I have compiled the next steps for you here.

Scan this code or head to the website to get any of the bonuses mentioned in this book.

Scan the code or visit:
launchedacademy.com/book-bonuses

🪐 CHAPTER 2

WHY RISK IT?

"You are here to build a business, not dream of building a business."

If you are already convinced you are starting your business and NOTHING will stand your way. Move on to chapter four.

If you need a pep talk about why you can and should start a business, keep reading.

It is okay if you need a pep talk, I am great at pep talks but DO. NOT. GET. STUCK. HERE.

You are here to build a business, not dream of building a business.

DREAMS ARE SAFEST AS DREAMS

We all have dreams; goals and plans that we want to achieve one day. We have dreams so big they make us pee a little. We have "maybe, one day" dreams, "when the time is right" dreams, and "as soon as things calm down" dreams.

Here's the reality, there is never a "right time". Life doesn't suddenly stop and get boring. Our dreams are not handed to us at the perfect time, with all the steps in order, and a big bow on top.

We have to go out and make our dreams happen.

Going after our dreams is scary as crap. This is why our dreams are safest when they are dreams. Taking the actual steps to start a clinic, write a book, or sell your crafts means you could fail.

If you fail at the dream, the dream is gone. So, we keep the dream. We talk about the dream, plan the dream, and dream about the dream. But actually taking action, that is hard. We could lose the dream so instead of risking failure we don't try at all.

CREATE YOUR DREAM

This is your call to try.

Do it!

This is your challenge to step into your dreams and make them happen.

We cannot live our lives afraid of what will happen if we do the crazy hard thing. You were called to do something. Let's do it. Stop being afraid of losing your dreams. It is time to live your life, create your dream. End the cycle of hiding behind the fantasy and step into making it happen.

It is time.

You only have one life, this is it! This is not a dress rehearsal. This, right now, this is your life, it is the only shot you've got.

It is time to see what you can do.

It is time to see what you can create.

A CAUTIONARY TALE

Several years ago I was taking a business course. An older couple in the group came to start their "one day" dream.

Their story is seared into my memory. Sear it into your memory as well. I even drew you a picture of the couple because visuals help you remember things. Never forget this.

The cute couple in my class bought a large piece of land when they got married. They wanted to use it to start their own business. They dreamed of hosting retreats. The whole plan was laid out. They knew about insurance, costs to get started, how to find their people, all the next steps. They were serious.

Then life happened. They needed to pay bills, they started having babies. It just wasn't the right time. They told themselves they would start the business when the kids were old enough to help run the place.

The kids got older, old enough to start helping, but the couple also felt overwhelmed by life. The kids had sports practices, music classes, parent-teacher conferences, and play practices. There was too much going on. It still wasn't the right time. The couple decided to wait until the kids were older.

The kids grew.

The cycle continued. At each new phase of this couple's life together they found something in the way of their dreams. They still planned, dreamed, and wanted this business but they never made the time in their lives for it.

They always found reasons to put it off for a few more years.

Each week I heard their stories of regret and frustration. I heard them make plans again. I felt hopeful and excited for them. Then I heard them say, "But we are probably too old now."

And each week, I realized my greatest fear.

> What if I never accomplish the things I dreamt of?

What if I die without a single check mark on my bucket list? I tried not to stare at them, slack-jawed as they told their stories. But inside I was in turmoil.

I promised myself I would not make those mistakes. I will not be in my late-seventies saying, "I wish I would have taken the chance. I wish I would have tried."

TAKING CENTER STAGE

> Your dreams are not patiently waiting in line for their chance at center stage. They are not primping and preparing backstage, waiting for everything else to take a turn.

You have to pull your dream out of the line-up and say, "This is it! This is what I am going to work on. It is your turn."

There is no perfect time. It is just you, your dreams, and the barriers YOU put in the way. That's right, I am saying it, the barriers you have are barriers you put there. You can take them down.

Sell the things you love to make, solve the problem, change the world. It is time. This is your call to take the chance. It is time to chase the dream. This is your moment to try. Who cares if you screw it up the first time?

It is better to take the chance than to never have tried.

🪐 MONEY, FUN, & ADRENALINE

The feel good part of my pep talk is over. Here is the "we all like money" piece. Here are five more reasons why owning your own business is kind of the absolute best.

INCREASED EARNING POTENTIAL

Typical nine to five jobs have income ceilings. There will come a time when you are at your max earning potential in your current job and there is nothing you can do about it. What happens when you hit an income ceiling and it still isn't enough money?

> The cool thing about business is that your earning cap
> is completely up to you.

It's your business, you get to choose the structure, how much you work, and how much of the profit you take home.

A well run business can give you unlimited earning potential. I want to say that again, a *well run* business can give you unlimited earning potential. If you are not running your business well you are very likely bleeding money instead of making it.

If a business isn't run well or you lack the foundation to grow and increase profit, it can cost a lot of money. Build your business with the right foundation, know your next steps (don't worry, we will talk about that). You can build an income source without an income ceiling.

Yay! Money!

MAXIMIZE YOUR TIME

I started working with a business owner about four years ago. She cried a few meetings in. She told me I was the answer to her prayers. God had sent me to her. She was completely tapped out, financially and mentally.

Jane had been running her business for almost a decade. She had never taken a paycheck. Ever.

^Yay! *Every business owner's dream.*^

She worked another job and her husband worked two jobs to support their family. Her business supported itself but added zero financial value to her life. In an effort to increase profits she expanded her building, a huge expense. In her mind, more space = more patrons per hour.

The trouble was, her staff couldn't keep up with more patrons. They were maxed out.

She hired me to fix the problem.

Together, we turned her family-run business into an efficient, well-run, fully functioning *business*.

> Within three years she went from never paying
> herself to grossing over 1 million dollars in revenue.

ONE MILLIONS DOLLARS!

She moved to another city while her business still continues to increase sales without her. Currently, she is looking at opening a second location. You can bet she pays herself now (and is doing much less work).

Well-run business = unlimited earning potential.

HAVE SOME FUN

Today, you have more opportunities than ever before!

The internet is amazing. It allows people to make money by doing what they love, no matter where they live. People in professions that have traditionally been associated with low income and constant struggle are finding their people online and killing it.

What do you love?

What could you happily spend most of your time doing?

Here is my first challenge for you. If you have the workbook, pull that sucker out. If you don't have the workbook, grab a pen and paper.

Write out your dream, answer the questions above and admit to the world what you want. Tell us what you want ("what you really, really want").

Set a timer. You have seven minutes to write it out. Do not overthink this. Do not hold back. Just write. I will wait here. :D

NERD ADRENALINE

Nerd adrenaline is my favorite kind of adrenaline. You might think I forgot my sarcastrophe there but I am dead serious.

There is something indescribable about the feeling of getting your first sale, killing a sales pitch, conquering a fear, or making a really cool spreadsheet. Seeing your profit go up for the third year in a row feels glorious. There is glowing, oozing pride in standing in your new, bigger office/store front and seeing what you have built. It is weird. But it is mine. That feeling is bottled up bravery, kick-assery, and just a touch of the middle finger to everyone who doubted you.

The entrepreneurs of the world get it.

There is an incredible thrill in creating your own business.

MAKE A CHANGE

Some of you reading this are good-hearted humans. I applaud you.

If you fall into the group of having the best of hearts, you might be wanting to start a business to change the world, or at least part of the world.

When you own your own business you can make change however you see fit. You don't need approval from your superiors. You don't need your projects approved. You are in control. If you think the world needs a place where mothers can learn how to teach their kids a second language, you can create that!

You are not beholden to everyone else and the things they think are important. You get to start that women's clinic, create eco-friendly products, and change the way couples communicate.

> No one can hold you back from changing the world.
> Go do what you were put on Earth to do.

🪐 BUSINESS BRINGS CONTROL

I used to be an employee. I wasn't a bad employee either. In fact, I was quickly promoted in almost every job I have ever had. I like to work; I like to boss others around. My employers saw that pretty quickly.

I learned pretty quickly that I hate working for other people.

I was a manager without the ability to choose my own team. My schedule was dictated by others. When I had good ideas they were often dismissed by management. I was somehow supposed to manage a team without decision making power that would have made me a better leader.

I hated answering to other humans. I hated asking for permission to use the restroom. I hated being told I had to work on Christmas Eve.

One of the greatest parts of running my own business is being able to work for me.

WORK TOWARDS YOUR GOALS (NOT YOUR BOSS'S)

If we are being honest, your boss's goals are very rarely your goals. Your boss does things too slowly, the dumb way, wastes a lot of time, puts all the work on you then takes the credit. ^What a gem.^

When you choose to stop working for other people and start working for yourself, you can run your business and your LIFE in the best way -- your way.

You get to set the goals, the standards, and all the policies. Think there is a stupid unofficial rule in your industry? Change it. No one gets to tell you what to do anymore, you are the boss!

CONTROL YOUR HOURS

Life was meant to be lived. After working as an entrepreneur for most of my adult life, going to an eight to five job sounds like actual Hell. I haven't worked a forty hour week in years.

I love that my family can visit museums, theme parks, and national monuments etc on a random Tuesday morning. Random Tuesday mornings almost always ensure we have the entire place to ourselves.

The ability to work my life around my job is a beautiful thing. I no longer live in a world where I force the important parts of my life to fit into the hours my job allows.

Imagine being able to go to all the things: kids' plays, sports events, weddings, a random week away, concerts, etc without needing permission from your boss.

I am raising a family. They will only be little for a short period of time. I want to be here for the things that matter to me. I want to be there for my people. I want to be able to call in sick when they are sick and do nothing but sit under blankets to watch all the cartoons.

GROW THE WAY YOU WANT

I have hated being in management positions with my hands tied. If I saw a problem that needed to be solved, I had to ask permission before fixing it. More often than not I was told to leave the big, gaping hole in the company alone. ^Because big, gaping company holes are better left ignored.^

When you own your own business you can do it YOUR way. Only want to serve three clients a week? Done. Want to add a new loyalty program? You can do that too. Ready to fix the big, gaping hole in the company? Go for it. Do it however you want. We both know your way was the right way anyway.

I have never played well with authority figures who I thought I was smarter than. I barely play well with authority figures who ARE smarter than me. Having my hands tied when I could see solutions to big problems made me feel certifiably insane.

My business will never run perfectly. However,

> Being able to make my own choices and create
> something of my very own was like finally being free.

BUILD AN AMAZING TEAM

When I started my first business I was afraid to do it alone. So, I called my friend, Caite, and convinced her to move 612 miles away from her home to start my business with me. We had no idea what we were doing. Luckily, we had a really great time (and sometimes very stressful time) figuring it out.

I have hired some incredible people to work with me. When Caite moved on to bigger and better things, I convinced my friend, Anita, to move 392 miles away from her home to run my business with me. Those are some of my very best memories. We had a blast together!

We road-tripped! We did big shows together. We sang in the car, met new people, and created an incredible business that we loved.

When you run your own business you get to surround yourself with those who build you up and make you a better person. You choose who you hire.

Never again will you be stuck with a coworker that makes you want to tear your eyes out of your skull just so you don't have to look at them anymore.

BRAIN FRIENDLY WORKFLOW

My brain is different from most people's brains. I lose things like crazy, I am a bit disorganized, an appointment that isn't in my calendar literally does not exist to me. I get bored really easily and can forget everything I am supposed to do in a single day.

I also have intense sleep issues. I frequently go 72 hours with no sleep at all. This is not a flex. My brain is the worst.

Creating my own businesses allowed me to create a life that works with my brain instead of trying to force my brain to conform to what others claim I should be doing.

I hate Monday. If I have an appointment on Monday, I will forget it. I never mean to. The intention to be at the meeting was there when I scheduled the meeting.

Here's the cool part: I don't have to work on Monday. I don't have to be at work at 8am on a Monday morning. Do you want to know what I am doing on Monday? Sleeping.

I am rarely out of bed before 9:00 am. I know some of you ^high power, super morning, sunlight is divine light^ types are choking on your 4:00 am coffee. Stay with me. It is okay that some people like to rise in time to see the buttcrack of dawn. I do not.

And I work for myself so guess what, I don't have to. Ta-da! Freedom!

Having your own business allows you to work with your idiosyncrasies. My entire business workflow was created to *compliment* my ADHD. *Massive sigh of relief*

I don't have to be like everyone else anymore. Imagine how good that feels.

🪐 BUSINESS BRINGS PERSONAL GROWTH

Business forces you to grow. When sinking or swimming rests solely on your shoulders, you learn to swim.

I know I am saying wonderful things about being a business owner. To be honest, it will be a cold day in Hell when I go back to eight to five work, W-2 employee status. I love being an entrepreneur.

However, business ownership is hard. There is no way around it. Entrepreneurship is hard. Half the time you don't know what you are doing. There is no boss or superior to go to when you don't know the answer.

Your success rests squarely on your own shoulders.

The weight of that responsibility can feel impossibly heavy sometimes.

BUSINESS OWNERSHIP IS HARD

The very best version of you is not cowering under a bush waiting for someone else to save you. The very best version of yourself is not waiting around for "the right time" or wondering if you are good enough.

Your highest and best self is kicking butt! Business ownership forces us to get to know that higher and best person a little bit more. We have to look in the mirror and figure out who we are and how we are moving forward.

Relying on yourself, having nobody to pick up the slack, forces you to grow. You gain confidence, trust in yourself, and so much resilience. All of those gains can be very painful gains. All of those things will make you a better version of you!

Business ownership is hard and that is where we find our best selves. Being an entrepreneur is like professional and personal development on steroids. You either grow, or you drown.

YOU WILL FAIL

Failure is a very tough pill for many to swallow. In my experience, women, especially, are very worried about failing. Sometimes failure can be catastrophic. You can lose millions. You can lose friends, family, homes, jobs, cars, etc. You can lose your dreams.

> However, most of the time our failures are a blip on the radar of our lives. It is a rare failure indeed that haunts us until the day we die.

You will make mistakes in your business, you will hire the wrong person, you will order bad products, you will screw up. You can recover from failure. Better yet, you learn and grow from failure. Failure is how we learn!

Failure isn't the end, it's the beginning of something new.

All of us failed at riding our bike the first time our parents put us on one. We all failed. We all got hurt, most of us cried. Many of us tried to quit. Much like riding a bike, business ownership is something we have to work at.

YOU WILL SUCCEED

If you never risk failure, you lose the chance to succeed.

You may stumble and make mistakes in your business, that is normal. Recognizing your mistakes and learning from them is what will propel you to success. You cannot succeed if you are not willing to try.

There are so many highs in business: making your first sale, getting an incredible review, beating a sales goal, signing a contract you never thought you were capable of, winning awards, meeting incredible people. Those moments are amazing.

These amazing moments fuel us to keep going. You have so much potential inside of you, imagine what it would feel like if you could let it all out.

If you never try, you lose the chance at all of these highs.

FIND YOUR HIGHEST & BEST SELF

The life of an entrepreneur is one that demands a lot from you. Personal development is an entrepreneurial requirement. Nobody is there to stand between you and an out-of-control client.

It's up to YOU to decide what kind of person you will be.

The journey of entrepreneurship teaches you how to become your highest self. Being an entrepreneur requires growth and development in order for you to not only succeed at what you do best but also teach others your ideas.

A successful business owner has much more than just money or material things going on inside themselves. They have a passion for what they are doing. They have incredible resilience, a drive for improvement, and grit to keep pushing forward.

Not all business owners started out this way. I bet most business owners started out scared and unsure. I imagine most of us doubted ourselves constantly. I imagine it was a roller coaster of a journey for almost all of us. It was for me.

We all had to find a better version of ourselves and keep pushing until we made it.

STAND TALL AND PROUD

When I was a photographer, I was asked to photograph a traditional Navajo (Dine) wedding ceremony. Some of the family was upset that I, a white girl, was there and was allowed to take photos of this ceremony.

I was doubting everything. I stepped out of the hogan to figure out my next move and probably cry, when an old Navajo elder tapped me on the shoulder. He had watched what was happening and followed me. He took me aside, looked me in the eye and told me, "You stand up straight and do your job! Everything will be fine."

I am sure he said other things, but this was the part that stuck with me. Stand up straight. Be proud of what you do. Square your shoulders and do not let other people make you feel small.

And I did.

I gathered myself, stood tall and proud and did my job. Everything was fine.

Over a decade later, I say this to myself often. Business seems hard sometimes. We all have haters and doubts. We can cower and let those thoughts eat us up inside, or we can stand up straight and proud and do the thing we *know* we were meant to do.

☺ BUILD THE LIFE YOU WANT

Tuesdays at the lake are the highlight of my life. Everyone is either at work or school. People have jobs, obligations, and are punching the clock. My family? We have the entire lake to ourselves. Well, it isn't so much a lake as a reservoir. But it is beautiful, it is quiet. If this isn't what heaven is like, I don't want to go.

My family takes the boat out to the dam, throws an anchor down, and we swim, eat, and relax all day. When we get bored we dive off the big rocks, tie the tube to the back of the boat, or pull out the jet skis. It's just us, the sky, the water, and the warm sun.

This is my dream life.

On Friday and Saturday the water will start to fill with other people. The dock is full of kids and sunbathers, so much so that it is hard to get our boat into the water. The other boaters make the water too choppy for my kids to swim safely. There is trash, noise, and humans everywhere.

I have Tuesdays -- goodness, I could have Mondays, Tuesdays, Wednesdays AND Thursdays if I wanted because I built my business to work with my life. I know what I want from my life so that is what I created.

YOUR DREAM LIFE

What is your dream life? We all talk about the life we want.

"One day, I am going to have a big swimming pool in the backyard."

"I am going to travel, that is my dream life, to travel more."

"One day I will get to see Paris!"

What are you hoping to have "one day"? What is the dream that seems so impossible you don't let yourself think about it often?

It is okay to have big life dreams. I think those dreams and hopes often keep us going. But I have a question for you, what are you doing to make your dream happen? What are you doing to *make* your dream life a reality?

YOUR BUSINESS SHOULD CONTRIBUTE

I like to reverse engineer my life. It is actually an ADHD hack. People with ADHD have a hard time creating the chronological steps of a project. In order to survive I started to reverse engineer my projects, in this case, my life.

It works like this:

1. What is my goal?
   I want to spend every Tuesday on the boat

2. What am I doing to get there?
   I am moving all of my meetings from Tuesdays

3. How do I move all of my meetings from Tuesdays?
   Block out my calendar, reschedule standing appointments

Sometimes getting something you want is just that easy. Sometimes, it takes a lot more work.

Oftentimes the only thing standing in our way is ourselves. If you don't know what you are actively doing to get closer to your dream life, you are the thing standing in the way of your dreams.

THIS IS YOUR ONLY LIFE

Approximately three weeks after my third child was born I realized I accidentally gave him the same name as a felon my sister used to date. I tried to ignore it and just let him grow into his name. I couldn't do it.

The name had to go.

My husband didn't want to deal with the paperwork so I promised I would take care of everything, we had to change his name.

That was two years ago. I finally did the name change paperwork two days ago. Do you know why it took me so long? Because I thought it might be hard. It seemed hard, it seemed like something I didn't know how to do so I put it off for two years!

We procrastinate our life goals all the time too. They remain hopes and dreams because they feel impossible. They feel like something only rich or fancy people could do. In reality, creating the life we want starts with something as easy as blocking out time on the calendar.

ADD VALUE TO YOUR LIFE

Your business shouldn't only move you closer to your dreams, it should also add value to your life. I used to be very good at working too much. I had big financial dreams in my business and I "needed" to get there. I needed to hit six figures. I was so close, I could feel it in my bones.

Six figures was my goal. My business was getting me closer.

However, this was not adding much value to my life. I was working all the time. I missed birthday parties, family events, even Tuesdays on the Lake.

As you start a business, you need to make sure it's adding value to your life. I believe entrepreneurship is supposed to give you freedom, not create a slightly more appealing prison. If you look around and realize your business is not adding value to your life, we need to talk.

The steps outlined in this book can help you fix that problem.

NEXT STEPS

Get your business started! Commit to your new adventure. San this code or head to the website to get any of the bonuses mentioned in this book.

Scan the code or visit:
launchedacademy.com/book-bonuses

☄ CHAPTER 3
FOCUS! FOCUS! FOCUS!

"My wonderful human, Pet Rocks exist. The founder of Pet Rock made millions - you can sell anything."

Making a commitment to start a business is the fun part. Brainstorming, planning, and imagining your amazing business is so exciting. It also leads to more business ideas, more plans on how to conquer the world, and more distractions.

I know you are excited. Exciting business ideas send a brilliant magenta tingle down my spine. I love them! It might be an addiction.

This is what makes choosing just one idea and

focusing on it so hard. But in order to get where you want to go, you have to choose just one. Here are some of the ways you might try to justify why you don't have to choose one.

I am on to you.

JUSTIFICATION ONE: "BUT, I HAVE SO MANY IDEAS!"

I know you have a lot of ideas. I do too. I have this s'mores restaurant idea that is going to be killer. One day. None of us have time right now to take on all of our ideas at once. Starting a business takes a lot of time. Starting three businesses at once is not impossible but all three businesses will suffer, as will your clients, you, and your family.

You are robbing yourself and your clients of a well-built business that serves their needs.

When we try to launch all of our ideas at once we don't have time to create well-rounded businesses. You slow your growth, your profitability, and your commitment. This is also a great way to help yourself burn out crazy fast.

Try this instead. Build one business to the point where it can run well, making money while you work 8 hours or less each week. Then start a new business. Repeat.

Let's focus on your first piece of creative genius. Decide which idea will set this world onto its feet and start there.

The same goes for all of the ideas you want to implement into your business. One at a time. Give easy ideas the chance to be amazing.

JUSTIFICATION TWO: "THIS ISN'T WORKING, LET'S TRY SOMETHING NEW"

I see this all the time with aspiring entrepreneurs. I call them "shippreneurs" because they want the dream so, so badly but they don't understand how to get the dream, so they jump ship after ship after ship looking for the "golden" idea.

My wonderful human, Pet Rocks exist. The founder of Pet Rock made millions. If a broke, freelance copywriter can sell millions of people a rock, not even a rock with googly eyes, just a rock, then you can sell whatever the hell you want.

Shippreneurs problems are not their ideas. It is a lack of sticking with their idea long enough to create the marketing to sell it. You will probably not become an overnight trend but you can sell your product or service, you just have to stick with it.

Every time you change gears to try another business or another idea, you have to start from the beginning again. Don't lose all your progress. Keep going.

JUSTIFICATION THREE: "THIS DOESN'T APPLY TO ME. I HAVE PLENTY OF TIME."

Imagine what you could do if you put all of that time into one business or goal. Think of how much faster you could move your business forward!

A few months into hiring my first business coach, I was telling her all about the new, exciting thing I was doing. She said something to the effect of liking my calls because they are so unpredictable.

Then, she told me I was not giving anything a chance. Every time I started to make progress on one business, or one new marketing idea, I would shift gears. She asked me how I ever expected to get to where I wanted to go if I wasn't willing to stay on the road long enough to see where it went.

She was the kind of coach that gave me all kinds of reality checks I didn't enjoy. 99.9% of everything she said to me was accurate. I *was* bailing before I even got started. I thought I had time to do it all so I would load my plate until there was nothing left, get overwhelmed, dump the entire plate and start again.

None of us have endless time. Time is our most finite resource. Spend that time well. Focus up.

JUSTIFICATION FOUR: "THERE IS MORE MONEY IN THIS OTHER IDEA."

I hate this sentence. It is a self-sabotaging sentence.

Each and every time a client tells me they are going to quit what they have been working on to start something completely new because they think there is more money in the new thing, I want to reach through my computer screen *(The Ring style)*, take their shoulders, shake them a little and say, "The money is right in front of you!"

This is not because I blindly believe every idea is a magical million dollar idea. It's because I have chased the bright and shiny things. I have watched countless clients chase the bright and shiny things.

Do you know where we all end up?

Right back at the beginning of our original business plan wishing we hadn't spent the last year of our lives chasing leprechaun gold when we could have been building our dreams.

JUSTIFICATION FIVE: "THIS WILL BE EASIER"

No it won't. All of it is hard work. All of it takes time.

I have done this a lot and I am here to tell you, everything only looks easier from the outside. Short term vacation rentals were one of my, "this will be easier. Quick cash." project. It was a pain in my butt. Sure, it didn't take as much work as a full time job but, it took just enough time to distract me from the business I was trying to build.

And it didn't pay very well. It was just a distraction.

(Plus you cannot imagine how picky some people can be. Someone was mad at us once because the toaster had some crumbs in the bottom of it. Do y'all check for toaster crumbs when you travel?!?)

That distraction took just enough time to sink my profits. It took just enough time and energy to make me batty.

It isn't easy. There are no easy shortcuts to creating the business we want, there are just barriers we put between ourselves and our goals. We put up these barriers to avoid the uncomfortable things we don't want to do. Barriers like a lot of distractions.

JUSTIFICATION SIX: "BUT I HAVE ADHD."

Me too.

Welcome to the club. We have jackets.

You have more distractions that you need to avoid than most people. Having more distractions doesn't mean you should give in to them. It means you are going to have to add some extra tools to your tool belt to help make sure you can stay on the road long enough to see some success.

These next few pages should be especially important to you. We are going to talk about tools.

ADHD can be an absolute superpower, but not if you let it run wild and free. Wild and free ADHD is how I ended up starting a cotton candy business with my kids instead of focusing on my business. That distraction set me back by six months in my business that was actually profitable.

ADHD is not a justification for denying your business the time it needs to succeed. I love you, but ADHD is not a good reason to jump ship, again.

TIME IS A FINITE RESOURCE

You can't redo your life. This is it. This moment, right now, this is your life. You are living it and you will never get this time back. Once your time is gone, it is gone. We don't get to be 21 again. We don't get to be 35 again. This isn't new and revolutionary information.

However, in my case, there was knowing it and *knowing* it.

I stood at my best friend's graveside about five years ago. I looked at all the people in her life, all the pain, all the worry, all the faces, and all I could think was, "What am I doing with my life?"

Everything suddenly felt so short. Life is fragile, ready to end at any moment. I felt this urge to make sure I made the most of it. I realized I was holding back on a lot of things, I wasn't taking a big leap. I was playing in the shallow end.

My life is too short.

> I don't get a do-over, you don't get a do-over. It is time to make the most of the time you have right now.

Time is finite; focus up and use it well.

USE YOUR TIME INTENTIONALLY

If you are going on this entrepreneurial journey your time just became limited. Limited time automatically means your time is more precious.

We often find ourselves exhausted by our children. They need more food, they lost the remote, they have another question, why are they eating dog food?! But, if you only had the weekends with your kid would that change your feelings about all the questions? What if you only had a day? What if you only had an hour a week with your children?

DON'T SUCK AT BUSINESS

An hour a week with the kids you gave life to? That time just became the most important and precious time possible. That hour with your kids would be vital, sacred, nothing would get in the way.

There are things in our life we need to guard time for. In the same way you would MAKE time to see your kids, if your time was limited. You need to MAKE time to create a business.

Businesses don't just fall into our laps. They don't raise and grow themselves. We have to be willing to dedicate some time, then guard that time from all of life's distractions.

ARE YOU ADDING VALUE?

What if you treated all of your time like it was that hour with your kids each week?

What if you were intentional with all of your time? What could you accomplish if you took out all of the time you spent doing things that don't add value to your life?

Sometimes we get stuck in projects or causes that don't add value, they just take time. Often the biggest "time-sucks" in our lives are the things we put in front of our goals.

For me, I like to do the "will-when dance". This looks like having a big mission, like writing a book, but deciding something else needs to happen first.

"I will write my book when I clean my entire house."

"I will write my book when I remodel my office."

"I will write my book after I reply to all of these emails."

I WANT to write my book, but I am scared of it so I put a will-when in front of it so I can push it off just a little bit. 365 days later I still don't have a book.

I just started a lot of dumb projects that took all of my time.

What would happen if you honored your time?

FOCUS ON WHAT YOU WANT – "WHAT YOU REALLY, REALLY WANT"

Social media is my biggest distractor. I want to watch that video. I need to know why that city is now a ghost town. ^I need to correct everyone's political views. They can't just go through life having their own incorrect opinions^. The distractions and my need for them are endless.

Hanging out on Facebook is not getting me any closer to any of the things I truly want in my life. As you attempt to direct your focus, you will have to remind yourself of what you really want.

Paint the dream, create a vision board, come up with a mantra. Why are you doing this? What do you get from it? What does your family get from starting a business? Where do you want to be in five years?

Focus on what you want, don't let the bright and shiny things along the path distract you. Get a coach or a mentor to help keep you accountable if you just can't help but chase the bright and shiny.

LEARNING TO SAY "NOT YET"

Part of focusing on where you want to go is learning how to say no. I have a list of ten questions I have to ask myself before I can take on a new project.

The very first question is, "Does this help me achieve my current objectives?" I have so many things I want to do. I want to do them all right now. I am impatient to see them finished.

In order to actually accomplish any of my goals I have to say no to other things. There is not enough time in the day to do everything. There is definitely not enough time in the day to do all the things on my massive list.

I am learning to triage my goals. I know which goals are urgent and important and which ones will wait on the shelf for a few more years.

> In order to reach our dreams, we have to say "not yet" to the little things.

CONQUER ONE THING AT A TIME

This section of my book has been blank for a long time because it's hard for me to finish one thing at a time. I am often a great starter. I can do the first 80% of a project with crazy, fast ease. But that last 20% is like walking through peanut butter, with my feet tied together, carrying 200 lbs.

It is hard!

Trudging through the end of a project is the only way I know how to finish a project. But finishing a project? Actually getting that sucker done?! That is amazing!!!

It drags and drags on you. It divides your focus. Having all those little projects in the back of your mind makes us feel like we aren't accomplishing anything. We have nothing to show for our work except a feeling of defeat.

Do what you need to do to get one project done at a time. Conquer your business piece by piece. This is part of why I created the Launch Your Business Academy. I needed a way to make business easier and give all my clients one thing to accomplish at a time. Step by step they are creating entire businesses.

AVOID THE VORTEX OF "BUSY"

In life, there is this crazy vortex we fall into called the Vortex of Busy. This vortex keeps us going and going and going while accomplishing exactly nothing at the same time. We feel busy. We are often completely overwhelmed by the vortex. Yet, when we are in the vortex our to-do list never gets smaller.

This vortex is what happens when we try to do everything at once. Instead of taking on one project at a time we take on all of the projects at once.

When we let this vortex into our lives, getting out feels nearly impossible. In the vortex, the only tasks we complete are the tasks that are the most urgent. We only focus on a task when it is nearly an emergency. In order to take care of these, "near-emergent tasks " we are forced to push everything else aside. And before we can get our feet back under us, the vortex sweeps us away again.

MULTITASKING IS COUNTERPRODUCTIVE

The first thing we need to understand when attempting to break free of the Vortex of Busy is, multitasking is a lie. We have been conned. Multitasking does not make us cooler, faster, smarter, or more productive.

Multitasking makes us slower, dumber, and less productive. I have no idea if it makes you look cooler, if it does, you handle busy better than me and my eye bags and frizzy hair.

According to the Harvard Business Review multitasking leads to as much as a 40% drop in productivity. (Bregman and Harvard Business Review) 40%!!? What could you do if you were getting 40% more done just by focusing on one thing at a time?

The same article also showed a 10% IQ drop in people who multitask vs their non-multitasking counterparts.

Be smarter. Stop multitasking.

TEST YOUR MULTITASKING SKILLS

I have a challenge for you. This challenge is specifically for the people who read those stats then thought, "But, I can multitask better than those losers." Prove it.

Let's see if your multitasking is slowing you down. Get a piece of paper and a stopwatch.

On both sides you are going to time yourself writing. You are going to write the alphabet then the numbers 1-26 underneath. It should look something like this:

A B C D E F...
1 2 3 4 5 6...

Here is the challenge. On the first side you are going to write a letter then a number, a letter then a number all the way to the end. You will write A then 1. B then 2. You will continue this pattern until the end of the alphabet.

Time yourself as you write as fast as you can. Write down your time.

Now, flip the page over. You are going to write the exact same thing but this time you will write the alphabet first then the numbers. Compare your two times.

Which was fast? Which was easier? Were you 40% slower when you tried to multi-task? I am 46% slower.

Multitasking is holding us back. Stop letting something as simple as focus, keep you from reaching your potential.

THE VALUE OF FOCUS

When we choose to focus on one thing at a time we tend to use our time more wisely. When we think we can do everything, we try to do everything and accomplish nothing. When we have to choose one thing to work on, we typically choose the most important.

When we choose focus, the most important thing gets done first.

One thing at a time also helps us feel less stressed. There is an urgency inside us when we are trying to do 10 things at once. When you set a timer and dedicate the next 20 minutes to one task you feel calmer, more in control. (Mark et al. #)

You also reduce mistakes when you focus on one task at a time. Little mistakes in your business can add up. Something as simple as dedicating time to one task at a time can save you crazy money. Yay, money!

If you do not know how to find the most important thing, I have some hacks on my TikTok for you (@launchedacademy). Go check them out.

MILESTONES MOTIVATE US TO KEEP GOING

You know the happy, little feeling you get when you cross something off your list? That feeling motivates us to keep going. Each little checkmark is a little hit of dopamine. Keep crossing things off equals get more dopamine.

When you focus on one, little task at a time your brain wants to keep going. Break all of your big (and probably overwhelming) tasks down into small, bite-sized ones. As you accomplish these micro goals and celebrate your victories you will find more and more motivation to keep going.

Whereas, if you try to do ten things at once and never get to the end of any of them, you feel discouraged and frustrated.

Focus up! What is your ONE next task?

🪐 THERE WILL ALWAYS BE DISTRACTIONS

I set a timer for 15 minutes so I could focus on this chapter. 15 minutes isn't very long at all. In those 15 minutes my six-year-old asked me to make him an egg. My nine-year-old asked me to read him Harry Potter. My 33-year-old husband came to lay next me to moan until I asked him what was wrong. I have had three texts, two messages, and one email.

IN FIFTEEN MINUTES

Your life will never be free of distractions (small family ones, or awesome idea ones). Your job is to learn how to say (to yourself and your people) "I cannot help you right now. Come back in fifteen minutes."

MORE OPPORTUNITIES IN A LIFETIME

"There will be more opportunities in a week than you could take advantage of in a lifetime." That is what my first business coach told me after a particular "shippreneur-esk" phone call. I had a new idea! I had a new plan! I wanted to try something different ... again. I didn't want to stick to the plan because this new "opportunity" was bigger, brighter, and shinier.

Just think of the possibilities.

When she told me there were opportunities everywhere I pretty much blew her off, ^Yeah, okay. There are opportunities everywhere^. But then I started to pay attention. There ARE opportunities everywhere.

There was also no way I could take advantage of all of them -- especially if I kept changing which one I was chasing.

Choosing your important is hard. Family. ^Obviously^.

But what else? Is family all that matters to you? What else is there? What is the most important when it comes to your goals and your dreams? What is most important in your business? What is most important in the world? What social justice issues do you need to support?

How do you choose?

How do you narrow down all the things that seem to be tugging at you and create a direction in your life?

BEGIN AT THE END

In order for us to make the right choices, we have to know where we are going. How do I get to France if I don't know France is my destination?

Where do you want to go?

I ask all of my clients to do this exercise. Think of your business 5-10 years from now. Really think about it. What are you doing? Who are you serving? How much money are you making? How much are you working?

"In five years my business will have served 500 clients, made $100k in annual revenue, and I will only work four days a week."

Now, what about in three years? How does your business look then? What goals do you need to hit in three years to set you up for your five year goals? Write it out.

Do the same thing for one year, six months, this month, and this week.

That is what is most important. Whatever goal you wrote down for this week, is the most important because it is directly related to getting you to your 5-10 year goal. The things you do this week will impact your goals in the future.

You have to know where you are headed to know which steps you need to take today.

☺ QUESTIONS TO DEFINE YOUR FOCUS

I will be the first to admit that even with my path laid out it can still be very easy to get distracted. I am a sucker for political causes and new business ideas. I like to get involved in the exciting things.

In reality, I don't have time to get involved in everything. I think I have time then I end up drowning in my to-dos while being sucked further and further away from what is most important.

I was explaining this to my life coach (yes, I need a lot of coaches to function. Don't judge me.) one day and she suggested I create a list of questions that I have to answer before I can get involved in new businesses. Or causes. Or riots.

Create a list of questions that address why you get distracted and if a new distraction is a good idea or a bad idea.

I once had a call with a different life coach and I told her I am too impulsive. She tried to tell me it was a really good thing and I need to lean into my whims. Now I have a cotton candy machine that lives on my dining room table. It's also bigger than my table. My family eats on the floor. FOCUS on your goals, not your whims.

These are my questions. Yours should be unique to you.
1. Did someone ask me to do this?
2. Do I have time to do this? Where is the time coming from?
3. Does this add value to my life?
4. Does this improve an important relationship that matters to me?
5. What am I giving up to do this?
6. How does this help me reach my important goals?

A DISTRACTIONS BOARD

I also have what I call a Distractions Board. This board is nailed to the wall next to my desk. I don't have to stand up to write on it.

Whenever I have a BRILLIANT idea (^all of my ideas^) that I just *know* I will have to implement one day it goes on the board. If it does not help me reach my current mission, it goes on the board.

Having it nailed to the wall is important. Because if it is a notebook, it will get lost. Having it visual is important. If it is a digital list I will forget it exists.

Putting my ideas on the Distractions Board helps me let go of them so I can focus on what matters. I have a lot of things I want to do in my life. I cannot do them all right now. You cannot reach all of your goals right now.

When I reach a goal and have time to add more, I go to the board and can choose what to move from the board to my current goal list.

ACCOUNTABILITY

This is my final tip for helping you focus on what is important. Find an accountability buddy. Better yet, get a business advisor you have to report to every week. The reality of being a human being? Statistically, most of us struggle to honor agreements with ourselves.

We are typically much more willing to let ourselves down than others. A study by the American Society of Training and Development discovered you only have a 10% chance of accomplishing your goals just by saying you have a goal. (Newland)

Committing to someone that you will accomplish your goal increases your chance to 65%. Having a specific accountability partner and reporting to them on a regular basis increases your chance to 95%.

Stack the deck in your favor and find someone that will keep you accountable. Meet with them regularly. Find someone that will keep you going when you want to give up or get distracted.

🪐 YOU WILL HAVE TO MAKE SACRIFICES

Sacrifice is required. Building a business is not like a typical 9-5 job. You don't get paid if your plans fail. You don't get paid if there are no clients one day. You don't have anyone to get your back if you fail. You can't ask for assistance from management.

Starting a business often requires more work for far less pay to get started. You will be stressed, tired, and terrified.

If you build your business correctly those things are worth it.

Understanding that sacrifice comes with building a business helps you keep your head up when things look less than ideal. This also helps you understand you are not alone. If you are struggling to get going, you are normal.

TYPES OF SACRIFICES

Some of the major sacrifices business owners face include an initial added stress and a big pay cut. Sometimes our businesses also creep into our sleep and family time.

We often forget we can clock out.

We keep working on our businesses even when we are home.

We also sacrifice things like office space and equipment. You are financially responsible for a lot and as your business grows you are also responsible for other people's paychecks!

Some of the business sacrifices are temporary. This is why it is so important to build your business correctly. We can make up that pay cut. We can get you your time back. We can create solid work/life balances.

There are sacrifices in businesses. I don't want to mislead you by claiming business is a sexy, fun, super glorious way to live. Sometimes it's the best. And sometimes you curl up in the fetal position under your desk and sob.

LET GO TO REACH HIGHER

When my oldest was about two years old we were at a local park. Being a two-year-old human he decided to climb up a twisty slide backwards. He was a little more than halfway up when he got stuck.

His arms were too short to reach around the next curve. His legs were spread as far as he could reach them. If he let go, he would fall back to the bottom of the slide, negating all of his hard earned progress.

Being a ^good mom^, I didn't rescue him. I sat on a bench watching to see what this two-year-old would do next.

He quickly understood the situation he was in and decided wailing for help was the only solution. From the top of the slide his dad reached down to help my two-year-old. He was like a cute, dad angel reaching out to save this kid.

My kiddo would not let go of the edges of the slide.

I listened to my husband, "You have to let go to get to the top. You have to let go."

ARE YOU STUCK?

It took several minutes of tears and wailing for my two-year-old to decide he could let go. He could take a risk and reach for his dad's hand.

This moment was incredibly profound for me.

How many times in life are we clinging to where we are and what we have even though we don't want it? Instead of reaching for the things we really want, we choke-hold what we have. Are you stuck halfway between your goals and where you started?

This little boy did not want to be stuck halfway up the slide. He wanted to reach the top.

The only way for him to reach the top was for him to let go of his "safe spot" and reach up. He had to risk falling. He had to risk slipping.

It took him ages to find the faith and bravery to let go.

WHAT WILL YOU LET GO OF?

When you are starting a business you will find there are things you are holding onto. These things are keeping you stuck.

Oftentimes these things are things like: worry that people will judge you, being comfortable in your current job, fear of failure, fear of success, or just fear of the unknown.

It is time to let all of that go.

What is keeping you stuck halfway up the slide? And what are you giving up by staying stuck in the middle? What do you have to do to let go and reach up?

Have the faith and bravery to let go.

ARE YOU READY?

We have covered so much in these first three chapters. If you are still on the fence about committing to your business, it probably isn't the right time for you. Focus on what is important to you right now instead.

If you are ready to build the business you have been dreaming of, let's go! The next seven chapters will outline the basics of your next steps and point you in the right direction. We are going to help you understand business foundations so you get the business results you want.

NEXT STEPS

Define your focus. What are you focusing on? What is pulling your focus?

Scan this code or head to the website to get any of the bonuses mentioned in this chapter. This will also help keep you updated on our next Launch Your Business Academy.

Scan the code or visit:
launchedacademy.com/book-bonuses

SECTION TWO
GETTING STARTED

🪐 CHAPTER 4

A THRIVING BUSINESS MODEL

"Prioritize TEACHING others your craft over doing it all yourself."

First up, legal stuff. Buckle up. We are going to do this fast and efficiently. Nobody likes the legal stuff.

Your business needs to be a legal business. If you don't believe me, here are a bunch of reasons why.

You business needs to be legal so you:

- Don't have your business shutdown by the government
- Are not charged back taxes
- Have a business name that is protected

- If something goes wrong your personal assets are protected
- Can do your taxes

All of those are good reasons to get your business legal. I cannot imagine why we need more.

Most people put off all the steps of making their business legal because they don't know what all the steps are. Some people don't like paying taxes. Others think that it's just too hard.

I am not going to lie, it often feels like it is far too complicated. But, you can get it done in a day. So just get it done.

That is all I have. You are risking a lot when you choose to run a business "under the radar". Please stop. If you are in the US you need to register your business with your state then with the federal government. You can find a free step-by-step guide on my website.

WHAT IS A BUSINESS MODEL?

Now we got that out of the way, let's talk about your business model! A business model is NOT your entity type. Your business model is how you deliver your goods and services.

Your business model determines if your business is all online, if your goods/ services are custom, how people shop with you, and so much more.

If you do not define your business model, good business decisions become complicated. To make good choices for your business, you need to know what you are building.

If you are a coach without a business model how do you determine what revenue streams are best to add? Do you only coach in person? Do you coach online? Do you teach classes? Do you offer group coaching? Do you offer courses?

Defining your business model at the beginning of building your business will help you answer crucial questions. A clear business model helps you know what you are growing and build it intentionally.

AIRBNB: OLD PRODUCT, NEW MODEL

AirBNB took the world by storm with this "rent any room" idea. Entire cities were changed by AirBNB (and real estate prices increased dramatically). It caused so much change some cities felt forced to ban short term rentals.

AirBNB changed the whole world!

But, the product, renting out part of your home, isn't a new product. Bed and breakfasts have been around for centuries. A home turned into a hotel, not even a little bit of a new idea.

The game changer was the business model.

AirBNB made it easy for anyone to turn their home into a bed and breakfast. They also made it easier for travelers to find these short term rentals. Combine those two things with the sense of security we all get from our rentals being "backed" by a third party company, huge success.

AirBNB did not invent a revolutionary product. They combined an old product with a slick business model.

CARVANA: OLD PRODUCT, NEW MODEL

Much like AirBNB, Carvana took an old product, added an updated business model and created an exciting new business.

Carvana is still selling cars. Carvana is a car dealership -- a used car dealership. What makes Carvana different and fun is its business model. We can now have cars delivered to our homes. We sell cars online and have them picked up from our homes. We have car vending machines!

That is cool!

And the thing that makes it cool? The business model.

If AirBNB and Carvana went into business without understanding what they were growing, these stories would have been much different. Instead of changing the world with AirBNBs, one city might have had an upgrade on short term rentals.

Instead of standing out with car vending machines, delivery, and pick-up, Carvana could just be one big car lot. One of many.

Your business model matters.

> If you don't know what you are building, you end up
> with a bunch of chaos you never intended.

MY PHOTOGRAPHY MISTAKE

When I was getting married, I had the hardest time finding a photographer. There were so many options! The prices and styles were all over the map and I had no idea how to even find them. It was a lengthy and frustrating process.

When I started my photography studio, fixing that process was one of my intentions. I had a dream to create this website where you could choose photography styles, your budget, and location and the website would spit out five photographers for you to choose from.

It was going to be amazing!

That was a cool business model.

However, I didn't understand it was a business model. It was just a vague idea I once had. I didn't take any steps towards it. I didn't create a plan, I didn't structure my business to support that idea.

I just started taking pictures, just like everyone else.

Ten years later, I was working endless hours. I had completely forgotten this dream goal and I was surrounded by a lot of chaos I never wanted my life to be. Without a solid business model I was just going with the flow.

I didn't know where I was going so I wandered aimlessly. I didn't know what I was building so I built haphazardly. Like a toddler. I built my business like a toddler plays with blocks, 'This one looks fun! Let's put it here!"

A BUSINESS MODEL HELPS YOU MAKE CHOICES

When you know exactly what your business model is, and you know what you want out of your business, you can make the right choices for your business.

Strategic choices. Growth choices.

Building a cute snow cone trailer for community events requires completely different steps than building a brick and mortar snow cone shop. Sure, the products are the same but the steps, assets, and tools are going to vary.

Building a physical and accredited tech school to teach people how to be a graphic designer requires completely different steps than an online graphic design course that teaches the same thing.

What is your business model? What are you building? How are you delivering your products and services?

DEFINING YOUR BUSINESS MODEL

Choose a business model! Let's break down how to define a business model that works well for you and what you are building. I put together a list of questions that will help you figure out where you want to go.

QUESTION ONE: HOW WILL YOU DELIVER YOUR GOODS/SERVICES?

"I let my business and perceived opportunities dictate my business model"

I used to travel for my work. Almost every single weekend I traveled hundreds of miles to teach business education. I didn't plan that, those were just the jobs I was getting. So, I took them. I let my business and perceived opportunities dictate my business model: traveling public speaker. Emphasis on traveling.

I didn't really want to travel and after a very close call with a rageful driver (not me) I realized traveling every week needed to go.

I created an intentional business model. I am building an online education company. I want business education to be available for everyone without having to travel to each person.

This business model means I don't speak in person as often. Instead, I am spending my time and resources to grow the online part of my business. I am growing an online business, online takes priority.

I am delivering my services virtually through online courses and one-on-one coaching. That is my business model.

QUESTION TWO: WHEN WILL BE YOUR "BUSY TIME"?

A lot of businesses have a busy season. If you are a landscaping business you are typically going to be the busiest through the summer time. Most product based businesses see an uptick in sales through the holidays.

If you want a business that thrives in the summer and gives you the rest of the year off, that should be part of your business model. Do more than hope it happens. If you want to do your best to eliminate ups and downs in your business, you will also need to make sure that is addressed in your business model.

My business, Launched, runs on a three month cycle. Every three months, we open the doors to the Launch Your Business Academy. That is a pretty crazy and busy month for us. I do well with sprints so I have selected a business model that needs sprints, but also has time for naps.

I don't feel comfortable with only opening my academy doors once a year. Annually is too much pressure on one event. I created a business model that allows my clients to get everything they need, without me needing to give 175% all of the time.

If you don't want to be busy at Christmas, create a business model that supports a lazy, cozy December.

QUESTION THREE: WHAT ARE YOUR LONG TERM REVENUE GOALS?

When we are talking about long term financial goals, your business model matters. Just trust me, your business model matters.

Simple fact, there is only so much you can do on your own. If you have a million dollar revenue objective, you will need people on your team to help you get there. You also need a business model that is scalable.

If your business model is simply, "I coach people one-on-one," you will eventually run out of time. What happens when your calendar is full but you are nowhere near your one million dollar mark?

For most business owners, this means a pretty dramatic shift in their business. EVERYTHING has to change in order for them to build a million dollar business. My hope for you is that you do not have to re-build.

Start thinking about this right now. What are your revenue goals? If you just want to make $50,000/year with your business, you can probably hit your goal on your own.

QUESTION FOUR: HOW WILL YOU GROW YOUR BUSINESS?

If you had a big number *(anything over $100,000)* for your revenue goal, you need to set your business up to support that right now.

I was on a call the other day with a Facebook ads manager. One of the first questions he asked me was how can my business support growth. Basically, if he gets me all the business he thinks he can get me, how am I going to be able to handle the increase?

If your business doubled overnight how would you keep up?

> What needs to be in place in order for you to double, triple, or ten times your business?

If you are a life coach and you only do 1:1 calls. There is a limit to your growth. Are you okay with that limit or are you creating something that will allow you to continue to grow?

You need to define all of this in your business model so you know where your business is going. Understanding your business model will dictate what you need to create, from the bottom up, so your business can reach the financial achievements you are aiming for.

QUESTION FIVE: ARE YOU BUILDING YOUR BUSINESS TO SELL IT?

I personally believe all businesses should be built so you can sell them later. What is the purpose if you work and work and work your whole life then one day, what? Just walk away?

When you retire, what is going to happen to
your business?

If you know, right now, that you plan on selling your business one day, you will build it differently. This is all part of your business model. If you build your business to orbit around you, if your business model is focused on you, it's going to be awfully hard to sell later.

BUILDING A BUSINESS TO SELL IT

Building a business you can sell is something many entrepreneurs never think of. However, I think it needs to be talked about. Knowing you can sell a business completely changes how we build businesses.

It also gives us an exit strategy. Let's dive into this!

Sometimes, when I teach about selling a business I have die hard, stubborn, my-business-is-my-baby-and-you-don't-sell-babies students. They are going to run their business forever and ever and no one will ever be able to replace them. ^That doesn't sound exhausting. At all.^

What happens when that stops being true?

Let's be real. You are not the same person you were fifteen years ago. You are probably not even the same person you were five years ago. We all change with life. We evolve, we learn new things. Our goals and our priorities shift with that growth.

In addition to your personal growth and changes, you will want to retire one day. Almost all of us want to stop working one day and just enjoy life. Why don't you prepare for that right now? What happens if you are physically incapable of continuing with your business?

When you reach one of those points, where you no longer want to continue your business or are no longer capable, there are only two possible outcomes for your business.

ENDING ONE: CLOSURE

The first possible outcome is closure. This can be a forced closure, like bankruptcy. Or a voluntary closure.

I had a sweet friend named Susan (name changed). Susan had the cutest gardening and flower shop. She spent twenty plus years growing this adorable and amazing business of hers. It helped so many people learn how to take care of our yards, save our trees, and create a better life.

Around 55 years old, Susan was diagnosed with cancer. Her health declined rapidly and the cancer was quickly declared as terminal.

Susan was forced to shut down her store.

> For months she liquidated everything she had worked for.

Her children met strangers and sold everything they possibly could, leaving nothing of Susan's life accomplishments but an empty, barren old building.

Susan didn't only have to shut down her store, she was also left with financial difficulties. She lost income. Instead of only having a medical crisis she now had a financial crisis as well.

At the time of her diagnosis Susan was working on preparing to sell her business. She understood the importance of creating a business that could run without her.

Unfortunately, preparing to sell a business when it has been built around the owner, is a very long and complicated task. Susan's cancer took her life before she ever had a chance to pass down her legacy.

ENDING TWO: LEGACY

The alternative option to shutting down is creating a legacy business.

A legacy business is a business that can survive without you. This business can be sold or passed on to another person.

> A legacy business can continue for lifetimes without you.

Building a legacy business is not an easy task. It requires foresight, intentional building, and a focus on business development over mastering your trade. This means, instead of focusing on being a better photographer, graphic designer, coach, jeweler, or whatever your craft may be, you are instead focused on how to build a business on a solid business foundation.

This doesn't mean you cannot be great at your craft or spend time improving your craft but it does mean you need to prioritize TEACHING others your craft over doing it all yourself.

If Walt Disney was the only person who could think up and create a Disney movie, Disney would have ended when Walt tragically died in 1966.

A legacy business is not a business that is centered around you. A legacy business is a business with a fully functional team. A legacy business has a scalable business model. A legacy business is a business with a solid and healthy foundation.

WHICH WILL YOU CHOOSE?

Susan's story seems like an extreme end to a business. It is a terribly sad story and it impacted me a lot. Susan knew the steps, she knew how to create a business she could sell. She didn't have enough time.

Unfortunately this is not a rare and unique story.

Business owners are frequently running their businesses into their death or sick bed. Worse, most do not have a contingency plan for what will happen to their business at the end of their lives. Many others choose to shut down when they reach retirement and still others are forced to shut down due to financial problems.

This is an important reality of business ownership. You will eventually exit your business. There is no getting around it. Eventually, you will exit your business.

The question is, what do you want to leave behind?

NEXT STEPS

Decide what type of business you are building. Are you building a lifestyle business or a legacy business? What will your business look like in ten years?

Scan this code or head to the website to get any of the bonuses mentioned in this chapter. This will also help keep you updated on our next Launch Your Business Academy.

Scan the code or visit:
launchedacademy.com/book-bonuses

🪐 CHAPTER 5
THE VALUE OF POWERFUL BRANDING

"Your brand is not your logo."

In the next six chapters we are going to cover six of the essential pieces of a solid business foundation. This foundation doesn't only help you create a profitable and sustainable business right now, it also lays the groundwork for a legacy business.

After your business is legal and you are confident in your business model, the next step is to create your brand. If you skip this part, you will eventually end up back here re-doing your branding.

If you have thousands of dollars in assets that are not branded correctly, you will get to redo all of those assets. Paying thousands of dollars again. For many businesses this mistake can cost an easy twenty thousand. ^Yay!^

Figuring out your business brand is first for a reason.

🎨 WHAT IS A BRAND?

Your brand is not your logo.

Your brand is who your company is: what you care about, what you stand for, what you like, who you are. Why does your business exist on this planet? How do you want people who come in contact with your business to feel?

That is your brand.

Your physical branding (colors, logo, fonts, etc) help carry the message of who you are in instantly recognizable ways. Your physical branding needs to be created with intention. You need to make sure your brand is sending the right message.

If you are not branding with intention, your potential clients will make their own assumptions about your company. Those assumptions will often become barriers to purchasing.

People are funny about branding sometimes. Branding sounds like a big mysterious thing that just pops up after years of business. ^Like magic.^ Sometimes people don't believe there is a difference between a brand and a business. Learning about branding can feel terribly confusing.

Let's simplify things.

Your business brand is your business's identity. Your brand is what your business stands for and cares about. Marketing is about your customer. Branding is all about your business. Your visual brand is where many entrepreneurs and designers get stuck. They mistakenly assume a brand is only the visual elements. In reality, the visual elements should exist to support the overall brand message.

Branding tells your customers who you are, what you care about, and how they can expect to feel when they come in contact with your business.

> A good brand allows customers to easily, and subconsciously identify how they fit within your business.

When I teach live branding classes we do an experiment. I show the classes a logo I created for Joan's Flowers. Then I ask the class what they know about Joan's Flowers based on nothing but the logo. Who shops here? What does this store sell? What type of people work here? What events do they serve?

I write all their answers on the board. Once they have told me all about this company, with no other info than the logo, I move to the next slide. The next slide is a list of the assumptions I knew they would make. It is essentially a copy of the class brainstormed on the board.

I know what assumptions the class will make about Joan's Flowers -- every time. This is not a guess, the logo for Joan's Flowers was intentionally designed to help people think those very specific things. And it works.

Our brains use visual cues to form opinions constantly.

> If you are not aware of what message your branding and logo is sending, you are sending the wrong message.

Have you ever gone on a walk with a toddler? It is grueling. Toddlers want to see, touch, and experience *everything*. They can spend fifteen minutes looking into a crack on the sidewalk, wondering at the world inside. When you walk with a toddler, a five minute walk easily turns into a 20 minute walk.

Toddlers don't have the same brain filters adults have. As kids grow up they develop filters that tell them what is relevant and irrelevant to them. As we age we stop noticing the things that don't matter to us. When you or I look at a tree we don't see each individual leaf, we see a tree full of leaves.

These filters affect how potential customers see our business. Without clear branding we can easily become the "leaves" our potential customers' brains deem as irrelevant. They won't even notice us.

How do you break through these filters and create a brand that stands out?

Brand with intention. Cultivate the message your brand is sending to your potential clients.

I once worked with a man who sold pre-packaged meal boxes. These weren't meal kits, they were pre-made meals you microwaved. His logo consisted of a big, burly caveman looking guy flexing his many muscles. His branding went along with the logo: big, loud, masculine, muscles.

He was frustrated because he could not seem to break into the "mom market". He wanted busy moms to buy his products for their kids. Imagine, a fridge full of easy, healthy, quick meals for your family. All delivered to your door each week.

The mothers were solidly *un*interested in what he was offering. He couldn't figure out what he was doing wrong.

The problem wasn't his product. The problem was his brand. Moms took one look at the big, mean caveman on the front of every package and their brains immediately said, "My kids won't eat it," and they never looked back.

Potential customers are not hanging around hoping to look deeper into your business when your brand clearly sends them the message that they don't fit. You have one shot. How do you stand out amongst all the leaves?

🌑 YOUR BRAND STORY

The first step to creating your brand intentionally is to know your business story.

Every business has an origin story. Your origin story may not be flashy or full of drama, but it does exist. Sometimes that story is about a family coming together and helping a brother learn to make the world's best waffles. Sometimes that story is just about wanting to run faster.

There is a reason each company was created. There was a purpose, there was a hope of return or improvement to a person or community. This origin story sets the tone for a business.

> If you know why your business exists you can help others understand why your business matters.

You have a reason you are in the business you are in. You could be building any kind of business. You could have chosen to stay at your nine to five job. You could have done anything.

There is a reason you chose the business you chose. There is a reason this particular business calls to you.

If you are thinking, "Because I wanted to make money," that's okay. However, you could have made money stripping, donating plasma, or being a scientific test subject. What made you choose your own business instead? What made you quit your job or go back to work? And most importantly, why did you choose *this* business? You could have chosen anything.

Take a long moment and write out why you chose the business you chose.

You may have been looking to support your family but what made your current business the business you went after? What do you like about your business? What do you hope to gain from entrepreneurship? What do you hope others gain from your business?

A lot of business owners will get stuck here. You might feel like you don't have the right answer. We often tell ourselves our story isn't good enough, no one cares, or "to make money" is a lame reason. ^How dare we want to make money!^

Many business owners feel like they need to make the story better before they can move on. Don't be like that.

You need the seed before you can plant the tree. Right now, you are just telling your imperfect, possibly messy, maybe even a little boring story.

Take down all of the walls. Tell the world why you chose to do this incredibly hard thing when you could have just stayed at home. Stop running away from your story and lean into it. You will be surprised at what you find when you stop trying to be what you think you "should" be and lean into what you are and why you are here.

> If you do not care about the purpose of your business, neither will anyone else.

🪐 YOUR BRAND MESSAGE

You have your brand story. Step two is to create your branding message.

Your brand message is your brand story summarized in one sentence. Think about how you want people to feel when they come into contact with your business. You know why you exist and what your business cares about, now what do you want others to feel?

Subaru is all about love. Subaru wants their clients to feel love and safety when they think of Subaru. Their theme is throughout all of their advertising, every commercial, every mailer I get in the mail, every ad.

Take another look at your brand story (I hope you actually wrote it) and see if

DON'T SUCK AT BUSINESS

there is a recurring theme. Do you want everyone to be happy when they come in contact with your business? Do you want them to laugh? Do you want them to feel like they have to sit up straighter and pay attention? Do you want them to feel like they are an exclusive and better group of humans?

Your brand message doesn't have to be for everyone. You cannot please everybody. It is not possible for your business to appeal to every human on the planet. Don't stress about it.

> Your brand message needs to speak about who you are, who your business is.

Some might call this a brand promise, or your "why". Either way, whatever you call it, your business needs one.

BRAND MESSAGE EXAMPLES

Here are several examples to get your creative juice flowing.

Subaru: "The Subaru Love Promise: Show love and respect to all people at every interaction"

LAUNCHED: "Bring hope and humor to women who dream of something bigger."

Coca-Cola: "To refresh the world and make a difference."

NIKE: "To bring inspiration and innovation to every athlete* in the world." *Followed by, "*If you have a body, you are an athlete."*

Fitness First: "Whatever you're aiming for, we'll help you go further."

Disney: "To create happiness through magical experiences."

BRAND MESSAGE VS MARKETING MESSAGE

Sometimes we get our brand message and our marketing message confused. Your *brand* message is what your company cares about. You should be able to put, "This company exists to..." before your brand message and have it make sense.

Your *marketing* message is what you offer to your target market. Your brand message doesn't talk about your products and services, your marketing message does.

For example, at LAUNCHED our brand message is: Bring hope and humor to women who dream of something bigger. That is what we believe. That is why I created my company. I believe a lot of women need hope they can do the hard things. I believe they can conquer mountains.

My *marketing* message is: Step-by-step business education that doesn't put you to sleep. That is what I offer.

I sell business education. Business education helps me accomplish my mission. Entrepreneurs having the tools they need to succeed, gives them hope and a real possibility of something bigger.

Take a beat and write out your brand message. You will probably adjust this many times as you create your company. That is okay. Right now, you just need something on paper. You cannot edit a blank page.

Pull from your story and in one or two sentences tell the world why your business exists and what you care about. It doesn't have to be planet changing.

YOUR VOICE & VALUES

The next step to creating a brand people will remember is to have a very clear voice. Your voice is how you present your brand message.

Let's say there are two companies with the same brand message, "To bring families together." This message can be presented in very different ways. Each way is going to attract a different type of customer and employee.

For example Mama's Little Bakery may bring families together by cooking a cheesecake so amazing people are willing to eat it off the floor. They have a sense of humor, they present everything they do with a tongue-in-cheek wit and a love that makes you want to hug someone wearing an apron.

Or perhaps you have a business called InGen that brings families together through daring recreational activities. They want your real-life dinosaur adventure with them to be an experience you will never forget. They are innovative, determined, and more than a little on the edge.

Both of these companies are going to present that brand message, "To bring families together" in an entirely different way.

How are you presenting your business? How are you presenting your brand message?

Are you funny? Sad? Loving? Edgy? Sexy? Weird? Loud? Clever?

STICK WITH YOUR CHOICES

You can choose a *max* of three voices for your business. For instance you can be weird, loud, and funny. You can create a brand all around your dorkiness. But being weird, loud, funny, sexy, and loving is confusing.

Choose how you want to make people feel about your company and stick with those choices.

Your voice will flow through your entire business. If your business is witty yet loving, you are going to need to recreate that feeling in your ads. Your employees will need to bring that voice into their daily interactions with customers.

This voice needs to line up with the graphics and copy throughout your website. We are not defining your message and your voice just for fun, this is an essential piece of your business. A piece that will help define what you create from here on out.

If you don't know how to be witty yet loving, choose something else. I know how to be sarcastic. It is a part of my soul, even when it probably shouldn't be. So, sarcasm is part of my brand. I can not only maintain those voice elements, I can also teach them.

> Your story, message, and voice are the heart of your brand.

This is how people will come to relate to you and connect with you.

Keep it simple.

Make sure you do not add too many voices. Do not flip-flop. Be clear and consistent. If your clients are confused you are increasing the number of times they need to come in contact with your business to remember you.

Don't forget to test.

> Before you commit to anything in your business, you need to do some simple marketing research.

Take your brand message and re-state it using the voice or feelings you chose.

Create a variety of options, put them out to the world. Put that brand message in your marketing, introduce your business to a new Facebook group using your brand message, use your brand message at a networking event.

Pay attention to how people react to it. Do they understand? Does it spark a conversation? Do they feel a commonality with you? Test your message to make sure it is clear. Use the results to nail down the core of your business brand.

⟨⟩ VISUAL APPEARANCE

Finally!! The part of branding everyone understands: how it looks.

I know you thought I was going straight to the logo but there are still a few more steps. ^Infuriating, I know^.

Certain visual cues make us think certain things. As a business owner you want to be intentional about your visual cues so you are sending the right message. If your brand is about saving the planet, you might want to shy away from fire-feeling visuals.

If you are a brand that embraces and celebrates the outdoors you might want to stay away from everything that makes people think of concrete.

There are three elements of your visual brand you need to be aware of.

FONTS

Font choice is important. When we see curly, cursive fonts we automatically think of cutesy, little girl things.

If your brand is a powerful, high academic brand, curly, cursive font is going to confuse your audience. If you are a high feminine brand for toddlers and you choose a font that looks very collegiate, you are going to confuse your audience.

Know what kind of font you are looking for. Sharp edges? Playful handwriting? Strong and firm? Feminine but not soft? What supports your message?

> All of the visual aspects of your brand are supporting players. They exist to help communicate and support your brand message.

SHAPES

Yes, your brand needs shapes. Shapes are a vital design element and they need to be consistent throughout everything you create for your business.

You need to intentionally choose shapes to help support your brand message. Do you have swirls and dots throughout your website helping customers feel fun and playful?

Consider our subconscious when you think of shapes. Humans in America associate circles with friendliness, kindness, and warmth. A rectangle makes us think of strength, solid, and trustworthy. A triangle is typically the shape associated with power and trickery.

Animators use these subconscious thoughts when creating characters in our favorite cartoons. Take a look at the latest animated movie! Do the personalities of characters match up with their shape language? (Walt Disney Family Museum) (Naghdi and Dream Farm Studios)

COLORS

Like shapes, colors have perceived meaning.

If Harley-Davidson's colors were a light pink and pale purple we would have different assumptions about who Harley-Davidson is and what they sell. That is just how our brains work.

Different regions of the world are going to relate different thoughts and ideas to different colors. For instance, in India a bride wears red on her wedding. In the U.S. a bride traditionally wears white on her wedding day. Red is going to create different thoughts for people living in India than it does for people living in the U.S.

Colors elicit emotional responses.

In small doses, pink has a very calming emotional response while red typically makes us want to move faster. The combination of yellow and red tends to increase our speed and our appetite. Sound like any restaurant chain you know of?

On the other hand, navy blue makes people feel a sense of trust. And green helps people relax.

When you are selecting the colors to represent your brand you want to make sure you are choosing colors that send your message clearly. If you are a rough and tough backpacking business, you probably don't want lavender and light teal as your colors. Lavender and light teal don't give off rough and tough vibes.

PUTTING IT ALL TOGETHER

There are endless ways to showcase your brand throughout your business. You have: a website, social pages, packaging, uniforms, emails, products, signage, videos, live calls, decor, etc. etc.

You need to ensure your brand flows through every aspect of your business. When customers walk into your brick and mortar or visit your website online, you want them to instantly know they are in the right place.

Analyze your physical branding. Does it represent your company throughout all of your assets? Is it consistent throughout all of your assets?

YOUR LOGO

Your logo should embody your brand.

Your logo, while not your brand, is incredibly important. It's also the last piece of your brand to be created. Logo creation is intentionally at the end of this list for a reason.

Logos should quickly and visually tell people who a company is, what they sell, and what they care about. Here are four things to consider when creating or analyzing your logo.

EASY TO READ

Your logo needs to be easy to read -- especially from a distance. You want potential clients to be able to read your logo at a glance. Accidental logo reading is the ultimate goal.

When I was a kid my grandmother had a big stereo in her front room, right by the front door. The cases of the CDs she had played would sit on top of the stereo.

When we went to her home we would sprint in the front door and race down to the basement freezer looking for ice cream cones. I don't think we even stopped to yell, "Hello!". ^Manners were clearly a high priority.^ I often found myself all the way in the basement, on the other side of the house, mentally singing random songs.

The phenomenon happened over and over again. I was singing Christmas music, I was singing church hymns. I couldn't figure out where this strange music came from. It wasn't playing anywhere.

It took me longer than I would like to admit, but I finally realized I was accidentally reading the CD case on my run through the living room. In those brief seconds my brain still read the titles of those discs and before I was consciously aware of it my brain was already singing the song.

Your logo needs to be *that* clear.

> Your logo needs to be so legible even a kid on a mad
> sprint for ice cream can read and understand it.

SUPPORT YOUR BRAND

Your logo needs to support your brand. If your brand is all about supporting women as they learn how to be mothers, it doesn't make sense for your logo to look like a nightclub.

If your brand is all about loving and embracing small communities and their rural economies it doesn't make sense to have a logo that looks like skyscrapers and busy streets.

Make sure your logo doesn't just match your brand but helps send the right message. If you are not branding intentionally, people will make their own assumptions about your business. ^'cause people never make assumptions about each other in real life.^ Oftentimes assumptions about your business are barriers to purchase.

True story, there is a bike shop a few hours from where I live. Their logo is a red pepper. The words, "bike shop," are barely visible to me. That giant red pepper is the first thing I see each time I drive by. I have pulled into that parking lot excitedly looking for Mexican food more than once.

I know I am not the only one.

Their logo sends the message of Mexican food. And it looks like it would be delicious Mexican food. I am disappointed all the time. ^Nothing makes you want to buy bike parts more than "hanger" and empty promises.^

What message is your logo sending?

EASY TO PRINT AND REPRODUCE

Tip number three: Make sure your logo is easy to print and reproduce. Eventually in your business (or possibly right now) you are going to put your logo on shirts, bags, packaging, letters, envelopes, or a book

The more complicated and colorful your logo is, the harder and more expensive it will be to add it to products.

When working on your logo you want to keep in mind what it will look like on printed products, signs, and packaging. A simple graphic is also easier for your clients to store in their long term memory.

PRIMARY & SECONDARY

I always suggest businesses create a primary and secondary logo.

Your primary logo is your full logo. It has your graphics, your business name, and usually a tag. The primary logo is bigger and busier than a secondary logo.

A secondary logo is like a stamp you can add to social media graphics, email signatures, your website icon, workbooks, packaging etc. This secondary logo is like the Nike swoosh, the McDonald's arches, the Facebook 'F', or the Amazon smile.

Secondary logos increase brand recognition without needing a lot of space. There will be many times in your business career where your logo just doesn't fit. Create your logo with a secondary logo in mind for these moments.

NEXT STEPS

Outline your brand. You will need to create drafts for your:
- Brand story
- Brand message
- Voice
- Brand elements and
- Logo

For more help and resources on your brand jump into a Launched workshop. Scan this code or head to the website to get any of the bonuses mentioned in this chapter. This will also help keep you updated on our next Launch Your Business Academy.

Scan the code or visit:
launchedacademy.com/book-bonuses

🪐 CHAPTER 6
FANS. FRIENDS. FRUSTRATERS. FOES.

"Create a business your fans flock to."

Your business does not serve everyone. The sooner you can part with the belief, "We are for everyone," the better.

You will never be the business for everyone. It is not possible. And that is okay. Sorry, it isn't okay. It is great!!

Human beings do not "fit in" with all other human beings. I am not the person for everyone. One size *does not* fit all.

103

> Your business does not serve everyone because you cannot put the entire human race into one box.

If you attempt to attract everyone, to make your business perfect for every human, you will fail. Pleasing everyone is an achievement no one on earth has ever accomplished before. Ever.

Christ couldn't do it.

Walt Disney couldn't do it.

The Ninja Turtles couldn't do it.

You can't do it.

Humans were not meant to fit perfectly into one box. Your business is not the exception. The sooner you understand what type of person you serve and how to serve them the very, very best, the sooner you can create a business your fans flock to.

🪐 FANS

You will have four types of potential clients in your business: fans, friends, frustraters, and foes. Fans is pretty self explanatory, these are the clients that love you. They love your business, they love what you do, they will wait in line for three hours in the cold to get what you sell.

These are the clients who will refer you, shout about you all over the place, spend good money, and move your business forward.

Your first step is to figure out who your fans are.

Look at your current clients. Who pays you on time? Who makes you happy? Who is the reason you started your business? If you don't have fans yet it's okay to imagine this person.

Give them a name. What do you know about them? We want all the details. How old are they? Do they have kids? Where do they live? What does their lifestyle look like? What do they love doing? What makes them laugh? What are they passionate about? Where do they shop?

The more you know about your fans, the better. If you don't know what your fans love or care about, it is really hard to attract them to your business. If you put out catnip you are going to attract cats. If you are looking for dogs and you put out catnip, you are going to be disappointed. Knowing what your fans like and care about will help you put out the right ads. Ads to bring in the right people.

If you don't have fans yet, don't worry. Start with identifying who you want. If you had the coolest, funnest, most amazing fans ever, who would they be?

It is important to mention here, you cannot forget your brand. Your brand is who you are as a company. If you throw your brand out the door to chase a trend it is the same as changing everything about yourself to try and please your boyfriend. Eventually you hate everything you have become.

Your brand and your target market need to overlap. You want to attract the people to your business who understand what you stand for. You want fans who like what your business does, and add value to your business and your brand.

Do not allow the people you "think" would be great in your business to dictate who your company is, what your goals are, and how you behave. That is a recipe for a fickle business who not only lacks substance, but also flip-flops to please everyone and, therefore, doesn't please anyone.

FANS MAKE OTHER FANS FEEL SAFE

Oftentimes, when we talk about a target market, business owners feel very anxious. Limiting who we market to? It can feel like we are turning money away. When you are just starting your business you don't want to say no to ANY money. You need the money, you take what you can get!

It feels very scary to say, "This is who I serve."

Here is the truth. Stating and clearly advertising for a certain group of people offers them safety. I don't want to show up to a Lord of the Rings party dressed like Spock. That would be awkward and even nerds can be mean.

I want to know what I am walking into. I always want to know what I am walking into.

> We want to know if they belong, what to expect, and how to act.

When you clearly state who your fans are, who you serve the best, you offer comfort for your potential clients. When we feel safe, we are more likely to take the first step. No one wants to feel like they walked into the wrong party.

Having this target market is not exclusion. I am often asked, "We are very inclusive in my company, so how can I have a target market?" Inclusion is fantastic!!

However, inclusion still doesn't mean you are the company for everyone. Something about you and your business will turn certain people away. Someone will find reasons to complain. Someone will decide they hate you.

That is literally how life works.

Your job is to find the type of clients who will absolutely love you, what you offer, and what you stand for. Then put out all the catnip that attracts them. If you are making sure you are inclusive of all races you get to include that in your description of your fans. If you want to make sure you are inclusive of all genders, that is part of your target market.

Some businesses do have a target market based around race. There are businesses that were created to help people of color, like makeup lines who go out of their way to have a range of dark skin tones. Or beauty salons who cater to people with coily hair. I have a client who specializes in teaching black girls how to become authors.

Sometimes a target market is specific to men, women, trans, or LGBTQ. In my business, my fans are women. I built this business to help women make the most of their businesses. Men are welcome to come along, but only if they are comfortable being surrounded by women (it is shocking how many men get all awkward and confused when they have to talk to women).

Your job is not to stand at your door making sure everyone is the "perfect" fan before they shop with you. Your job is to understand who your best and brightest fans are and intentionally create the marketing that attracts them.

I was teaching a class several years ago and a business owner raised his hand. He takes adventurers on paddle board excursions. He told me he could not afford to have a target market because he needs everyone. He needs every penny.

"Cool. Tell me who you like to work with the very most. Who do you like to take on these paddle board excursions?"

"Experienced paddle boarders. When we have beginners they can't keep up, we spend a lot of time teaching them, and it holds everyone else back."

"Swell," I responded, "How is that creating a great experience for any of your clients?"

What this man had accidentally done in his fear of declaring a target market is create a frustrating experience for all of his customers. Not knowing what to expect, newbies signed up for this excursion. What they were met with was feeling foolish and frustrated while they struggled to keep up with the group. They were panicking about learning a new skill while everyone else impatiently stared at them.

He also hurt the experience of the advanced paddle boarders. Not knowing exactly what they expected, they signed up for an exciting and adventurous paddle boarding experience. What they got was a lot of waiting around for other people, not being able to complete the trip in the amount of time they wanted, and feeling frustrated about being held back.

How does this create loyal customers?

How does this impact online reviews?

The beginners and the advanced paddle boarders needed to know what to expect from the tour company. They needed to know what skills were required and what type of people make the trip. They needed to know if they belonged.

We all need to know if we belong.

> A target market feels scary for business owners. It is safety for your clients.

It is twice as expensive to try and attract two different target markets. It can also be confusing to your audience. Are you for newbies? Do you serve chocolate or peanut butter? Will my family be too loud? Focus on one target market.

FRIENDS

You now know all about fans and why they matter in your business. But what about the other three types of potential clients? What do you do with everyone else?

Friends are the second type of potential client you will often encounter in your business. These are the customers that spend a little bit of money. They like some of your posts, think you are doing good things, and are happy to be along for the ride. However, friends are not driving your business forward.

Your friends like freebies, great deals, and the general atmosphere of your business. Even though they are not big spenders they can still take a lot of time. You still love these friends. Friends add to your business and support your fans but they should never be your top priority.

There are three rules for managing friends in your business: never chase them, create a friend package, and be happy they are a part of your business.

A friend package is a service or product that is low cost, takes very little of your time, and encourages your friends to stick around and come back for more. Create an easy-to-make, low cost item or service to keep your friends supported and make them feel loved but that doesn't take all of your energy and resources.

This offer should take very little to zero of your time.

If you are a coach, it might be a pre-recorded class. It might be a group call. If you sell products this could be a simple and cheaper product. Find the core product specific to your friends. Create something that allows them to spend money with you within their smaller budgets.

Remember, you are building your business for your fans, not your friends

We are not writing off our friends. They are good humans who support the overall mission of our business. They are adding value to the atmosphere. They add value to your fans. They are an asset. We want to keep them hanging around. You want their support.

Friends can turn into fans! When we support and love our friends, they can decide if they want to take the next step with our company.

Maybe they are finally ready to try our most expensive item. Maybe they are finally ready to ditch our competition. ^We were the clear better option anyway.^ There often come times in the customer journey when a customer hangs out in the friend zone for a long time. They are looking at their options, weighing the benefits, gathering their nerves.

> It is okay for potential clients to hang out in the friend zone.

You get to give them what they need while they are in the friend zone and give them the path to take the next step.

FRUSTRATERS

Frustraters are the clients your business doesn't have the capacity to manage. They are too big. They might look exciting and fun and sometimes even life changing, but they put your business in a risky position.

There are a few things that classify a client as a frustrater.

If one client is more than ¼ of your business they are typically a frustrator. Too much of your business success rides on them. What happens if they leave? Do you really want more than ¼ of your income depending on the decisions of one person?

Frustraters can be so big you don't have room for mistakes. While the revenue might be big when you are working with a frustrater, the profit margin is very small.

Many business owners dream of having their products in big box stores. If your products are in the biggest box stores you have made it. It can be crazy exciting to finally get that deal!

While a deal with a big box store can be the Holy Grail for some business owners, it is the false grail for others. This means, while the grail looks shiny and wonderful, drinking from it will force your business to prematurely meet its end.

So, what's the difference?

The businesses who find success in big box deals are businesses who are ready for big box deals. These are businesses that have fantastic systems. They have the finances to be able to float a massive order for up to three months. Yes, three months. Big box stores can have up to a net 120 as a payment agreement. They will pay you, 120 days after you deliver.

Businesses who find that their big box store Holy Grail was really a false grail are businesses who weren't yet prepared for massive clients. They didn't have the cash flow to float giant orders and they didn't have the systems to get these orders done in a timely manner. Taking on a massive client, like a big box store, completely halts and frustrates everything in their business.

> We often see these big clients and enthusiastically jump before determining if our business will survive the fall.

I have a friend who used to own a popcorn shop. His store got a very, very large order from a company in New Orleans. He was elated. It was big money.

My friend knew his numbers very well. Before jumping he analyzed this order and what it would mean for his business. He realized this flashy order was too big. If everything went perfectly he would make some good money.

However, if there were any mistakes his company would end up losing a lot of money. His team made mistakes sometimes, they were human beings. Typically, the cost of mistakes was worked into his prices. Because this order was such a high bulk order and the buyer wanted a deal for the massive volume, there wasn't enough of a profit margin for his team to make *any* mistakes.

He also realized he would have to put all other production on hold, he would have to delay fulfillment for regular clients. Fulfilling this order would require all his business resources and focus to go into getting this order perfect.

The halt in all other production meant there was even less of a financial buffer if things went wrong.

With one mistake his business could go from making life changing money to sinking deeply into the red. He wisely turned down the deal.

We get stars in our eyes when the frustraters come calling. Part of your job as a business owner is to know when your business can take a risk and when a risk is more than your business can handle. Frustrater clients put businesses under all of the time.

Look at your business and identify your frustraters. If you have not opened your doors, you still need to know what you are looking for. If you have never had a frustrater client, now is a great time to outline what they would look like for you.

A frustrater is going to be someone who halts production/services for almost everyone but them. They are gumming up your systems and processes. They alone could make or break your business. If they fire you, your business would be over.

How will you know frustraters in your business? Who might they be? Knowing them before they get to you, is a massive benefit. You will already know how to handle the situation.

It is worth mentioning that you can grow into your frustraters. For a lot of businesses their goals include being able to take on bigger clients.

It is okay to tell the frustrater clients you are not a great fit for them, right now. Maybe you can't take a tour bus of 200 people right now, but maybe you can in a few years. Maybe you can't fill a quarter of a million dollar order today, but maybe you can soon.

As your business continues to grow and you increase capacity and improve your systems, you may be a perfect fit for your past frustraters. Keep their information and reach out to them as your business is capable of more.

You want a sustainable business that can weather hard times. You want a business that can survive when a client moves on, or closes their own business.

Sustainable means *not* being reliant on frustraters.

If you are realizing you already have a frustrater in your midst, don't panic. Your next steps are to start working yourself out of this situation.

That can look like simply firing the frustrater and sending them on to an associate. You can behind to increase capacity so you can take on more clients, keep your frustrater from controlling the bulk of your business. It can also look like taking on smaller clients to start replacing the frustraters income so you can fire them.

Firing a frustrater is quite simple. You just say, "We are so happy you considered us for this project. At this time we don't have all the resources we need to be able to confidently fulfill your order. We will keep you in the loop as our business continues to grow. Here are two businesses that might be able to help instead..."

Don't lose sight of who you are building your business for. If you fill your business with frustraters because they look sparkly and fun, you will never have room for your fans.

🪐 FOES

Up next we have the foes in your business. A foe is exactly what it sounds like.

A foe only contributes to causing chaos and problems in your business. Foes do not help you reach your goals, they often hold you back from them.

These are the people who refuse to pay you, always want refunds, scream at you on the phone, leave terrible reviews, and make everyone within your business feel anxious and uncomfortable.

If you get an email from a client, see their name, and think, "I just don't have time for their crap today!" You have a foe.

These clients actively work against your progress. This is the guy screaming at you over the register. This is the woman who always wants a steep discount or she will "ruin you."

Foes are clients who are never happy, take all your time and energy, and rarely *(if ever)* pay you in full. These are not just people looking for a bargain, these are people willing to watch your business fail in order to get what they want.

Fire your foes.

Politely but firmly send them somewhere else.

I managed a pizza place when I was sixteen. One evening I was making dough in the back when I heard a ruckus in the front of the store. I checked my register only to find my front desk girl in tears while some big man loomed over her, yelling.

He was furious because the prices on the board and the price he was charged was off by two or three cents according to his tax calculations. Every family in the restaurant had stopped to watch Crazy Guy scream at my cashier, who didn't have the ability to re-open the register.

Every customers' meals and experience were tainted by this foe, screaming at everyone for three cents.

I catered to Crazy Guy. I probably comped his meal or gave him a free drink or a free dessert. I didn't apologize to my regulars. I didn't do anything for those fans trying to enjoy their meal. I apologized to Crazy Guy, effectively throwing my employee under the bus and solidifying the already tense atmosphere in the restaurant.

The people you allow into your business set the tone and atmosphere for everyone else.

In the situation with Crazy Guy, I should have apologized to the fans, the regulars already eating. They all should have got free desserts. I should have backed up my employee instead of throwing her under the bus.

I should have refunded Crazy Guy and sent him next door. I should have let him know he was more than welcome to shop somewhere else, but if he was going to eat in our restaurant he needed to calm down.

So many times in business we allow the foes to have the control. We let them suck our energy, our resources, and our time. We allow foes to negatively impact everyone's experience. It is time to stand up to your foes.

As a leader you have an obligation to your people.

Your employees and team don't deserve to be subject to the ragings and abuse of your business foes. Your fans and friends don't want to continue to frequent a business that makes them feel uncomfortable or unsafe.

Fire your foes.

The fire-your-foes script goes, "I don't think we are going to be a great fit. Here are some other businesses who might serve your needs better," or even "Sir, you need to leave."

As you build your business you want to remember who your foes are and who your fans are. Everything you say, all of your ads and social posts, should appeal to your fans and repel your foes.

You need systems in place that help you avoid the foes from the very start.

Great systems that help you avoid foes include things like: payment due up front, non-refundable deposits, carefully crafted questionnaires, solid work hours, holding your boundaries and business policies, etc.

Foes look for ways to get around the rules. Hold your ground. Create systems and policies that protect you and your employees. Sometimes a good boundary is all it takes for a foe to either shape up or choose to prey on someone else.

DON'T SUCK AT BUSINESS

A few years ago one of my clients had a foe in her business. This woman was never happy. Picky Polly was mad about everything. She was mad when the business owner didn't answer the phone at 8:00 pm. She was mad when she had to approve custom orders. Nothing was good enough.

I advised my client to let her go.

My client had the breakup talk with Picky Polly and suddenly Picky Polly started singing a different tune. She apologized for not understanding how the business ran. She apologized for not trusting the business owner. She checked herself and quickly became a fan instead of a foe.

*Do not be af*raid to stand up to your foes. Some of them will tell you that you suck and find someone else. Let them go. Others will realize what it costs to lose you and transform like a butterfly.

🪐 YOU ARE A LEADER. LEADERS PROTECT.

Whether you like it or not, being a business owner makes you a leader. You are leading your business, your team, and your customers.

The role of a leader is not only to guide but to protect. We have all worked with that crazy, toxic person our boss refuses to fire. They let them hang out for ages while they drive good team members away.

> The lack of backbone is the sign of a weak leader.

A good leader understands how one foe can drive away the fans. One toxic employee can drive away great ones. A good leader protects their people from crappy situations. A good leader protects the environment and the culture within their organization.

If you are allowing frustraters to take all of your time and business resources, you are not protecting your fans. You are throwing their needs under the bus.

They are willing to go to bat for you, they are driving your business forward, and you are pushing them aside for a risky shot at a big payout.

If you are allowing foes into your business you are creating an unsafe environment for your fans and your team. Nobody wants to be in a restaurant when Crazy Guy is screaming at everyone.

Somehow, as business owners our instinct is to appease Crazy Guy. Make him happy. Give him whatever he needs. We put all our time and energy into Crazy Guy when it should be going to our fans.

Years ago I was in a pretty high dollar business program. Part of that program was a monthly group coaching call.

One month I got on the *call and* they had added a new man to our group. Within 30 seconds he was screaming at the host. I mean, screaming. He wasn't asking questions. He wasn't mildly frustrated, this guy was pissed and he wanted everyone to know. None of us on the call had any idea what set him off. Screaming Steve came to the call to pick a fight.

The host handled Screaming Steve well. She was very kind and considerate and tried to address all of his issues. He interrupted everybody. He talked over the host when she tried to offer us advice. It was a shit show. But the host was always kind and calm.

This was great customer service. Good for her for keeping her cool.

But this wasn't great leadership.

Screaming Steve took over our entire meeting, a meeting we paid thousands for. He was the focus of the entire call. He took over everything and no one else's needs were met.

The rest of us on the call were the fans. We wanted to be there, we loved this program, we were dedicated. Screaming Steve was the foe and true to a foe's nature he ruined the experience for everyone else.

How much more loyal would we have been if the host simply booted him out of the call and said, "You ladies don't deserve to have your time and experiences destroyed by that. I will attend to his issues later but I want to take care of you right now."? Holy cow!! That would have been amazing! She would have earned our loyalty for life.

When you find yourself hesitating to fire your foes and frustraters remember what you are choosing by keeping them. You are choosing to give your time and energy to the worst clients in your business. You are choosing to negatively impact the experience of your fans and friends.

You are choosing to contribute to driving away your favorite people in your business.

Loyalty is powerful.

You want to keep the good clients in your business. You don't want to find new ones, you want to keep the people you have for as long as you can keep them. Finding new clients costs five times more than retaining the ones you already have. (Rioux and Forbes) You are also 14 times more likely to sell a current client on a new product or service than convert a new client. (Farris #)

The stats go on and on. Retaining current customers makes your business significantly more money than constantly sourcing new customers. Make sure you are focusing your business, time, and energy on the right people. Do you really want to retain your foes? Or do you want to multiply your fans?

> Loyalty doesn't just lead to return clients. Loyalty leads to increased spending, great testimonials, and increased referrals.

Loyalty, especially fierce loyalty can dramatically change the landscape of a budding business.

Fire your foes. Focus on your fans. Prioritize who you spend time on. Earn endless loyalty.

NEXT STEPS

Define your target market. Know your:
- Fans
- Friends
- Frustrators and
- Foes

For more help and resources on defining your customer categories, jump in a Launched workshop. Scan this code or head to the website to get any of the bonuses mentioned in this chapter. This will also help keep you updated on our next Launch Your Business Academy.

Scan the code or visit:
launchedacademy.com/book-bonuses

☄ CHAPTER 7

BRINGING YOUR FANS INTO YOUR ORBIT

"No one has time to chase every single prospect."

We know who your fans are and why they deserve to be at the very top of your priority list. We also know who you don't want to work with and have agreed to send the foes packing. At least I hope you have agreed. ^If you are still holding onto those foes we might need to get you a therapist.^

Stop loving people who treat you badly!

Let's talk about how to find those amazing and sometimes elusive fans.

In the Launch Your Business Academy we talk a lot about watering holes. A watering hole is a place where animals gather to slake their thirst.

Your fans have watering holes as well. They may not always be quenching their thirst at their watering holes, but there are places where they gather.

What do you already know about your fans? Where these types of people hang out. What brings them together?

You can definitely go out and find your fans one at a time. Many new business owners do. However, if you can reach 20 fans at one time, you just 20x the reach of your marketing without having to do much more than you would have for that one-on-one.

My very first business was a photography studio. I was a professional wedding photographer and I was very good at it. I often hired second shooters to come help me with weddings. I remember hiring one girl, we will call her Suzy, who had been in business for about ten years.

She was confused that I had already been published in bridal magazines and I was only two years into my business. Suzy was floored that my studio was booked out for the year and most of the next year. She was in awe with the exclusive venue where we were shooting.

I didn't realize until I met her that I was an anomaly. I didn't do all the things other photographers did. I didn't follow the written path, I didn't "pay my dues" or work my way up.

I found exactly where my audience was and went and camped out in front of them. I bought booths at massive bridal shows. Most couples get engaged between October and January so I went to shows in January. I stood right where my brides were and sold my services. I could write a whole other book on how to build a sustainable business from shows and expos.

I got my photos and weddings published in bridal magazines because I submitted them everywhere. I knew where my market was and I was dedicated to being directly in front of them.

We often spend too much time chasing the one-to-one sale. We see one bride get engaged online and we pounce, "I'm not a crazy person but I take pictures. I see you just got engaged. How was it? Do you have a photographer? Here's my portfolio, I can totally take your pictures."

Not only is this overwhelming for potential customers ^cause everyone loves a pushy and insane business owner^ it is also overwhelming for us! Do you know how many brides I would have had to accost to book out a year of weddings? Over one hundred. One hundred crazy person interactions over a year. Every three days I would have to be out there begging brides to take me, searching the internet and the popular engagement locations for any hints of a new ring.

^Sounds super fun and exciting. I probably would have only been arrested a handful of times.^

This is why we find watering holes.

No one has time to chase every single prospect. The one-on-one chase makes us feel desperate and discouraged.

Occasionally, you can find a fantastic watering hole, all your fans are there, their friends are there, they are everywhere! So, you target that watering hole, you send out all the ads, you start networking, you put up signs, maybe even a booth. But, nothing works. In fact, some people are simply hostile.

You are the alligator at the watering hole. You found a watering hole, sure, but instead of showing up as another friendly animal, you showed up as an alligator. This happens when you are not paying attention to the reason people are gathering.

Sometimes your fans are gathering where it would be inappropriate to advertise your services.

I can be a super horror movie fan. But a creepy, horror movie trailer played

122

before a kids' movie isn't going to win me over, it is going to make me mad. Now you have made my kids cry and possibly ruined our evening. An evening I paid for and probably fought my kids to enjoy.

I was looking forward to shoving my face with the world's most terrible-for-you popcorn, and now, instead I get to ^enjoy^ standing in the hallway while my kid cries because you couldn't read a room.

Not only am I un-excited to see your horror movie, now I will actively protest it.

If a bunch of business women gather in the park to do yoga and you show up to sell business insurance, the yogis are not going to give a downward-facing-dog. They are not in the park doing yoga because they secretly wanted to learn more about insurance. They are in the park doing yoga because they are looking for some peace.

A juice bar could sell them something. You, an insurance agent, cannot.

It is like when your kid comes to you the second you sit down on the toilet and starts asking through the door if they can have a hug. Dude, I will always be here to hug you but I. AM. BUSY.

Make sure you are choosing watering holes where your fans are most primed and receptive to your message.

None of us want to be the pushy salesman. There are three reasons we typically feel sales people are too pushy.

They are not listening.

They do not care about who they sell to.

They are only focused on their product.

Once you find your watering hole, you want to be actively selling your business, but in order to do that you need to stop selling and start listening.

Start your sales pitch with questions.

Ask the probing questions. If you are marketing a horror movie ask them which horror movie was the last one they saw. Did they like it? What is their favorite genre? Would they like to hear about an upcoming one they might love?

Now you are having a conversation. Now you are creating a relationship. Just by asking questions you are listening, not selling immediately, and focusing on the person instead of your product.

As a wedding photographer in a booth at a massive show, I did three things.

Started the conversation with a compliment, "Hi! I like your shoes!"

Asked three questions about them, "When is your wedding?", "What part of your wedding are you most excited for so far?", "What venue did you choose?"

Gave them an irresistible offer, "I am a wedding photographer, my name is Kara, and I am giving away free wedding photos today. Do you want to enter to win?"

An easy 85% of brides entered to win. From that one day of interactions I could easily book a year and half of weddings.

FANS LIKE

The best way to figure out how to start a conversation with your fans is to understand what they need.

Think of your business like a planet. You are creating this planet, almost a getaway, for your fans. You don't want to just give your fans a product, you want to give them an experience. You want to give them a place where they are safe, welcome, and want to return to again and again.

In order to do this well, you need to know what your fans like. What do they do with their families? What do they do to kick back and relax? What makes them smile? What do they like to spend money on? What are they suckers for every, single time? Where do they want to spend their time?

Think of your very favorite client and write down everything you know about what they like. Get to know them. If you don't know the answers, call them and ask if you can interview them. Take them to lunch and tell them you want to know your customers better.

Learn what your fans like so you can customize an experience for them.

I am a 90's kid. A business who makes good 90's references, always has my attention. 90's kids (like every generation) have things we love -- and things that will send us running for the hills. You want to include the things your fans like your marketing.

If your fans are women with small children, you might want to incorporate kids into your marketing. You don't want to show a single, childless woman who has no cares in the world in your marketing. Your fans won't connect with her.

If your fans are Christians you are allowed and encouraged to mention God in your marketing.

Understand what your customers like so you can connect with them immediately. You turn your ads into a Fresh Prince rap parody and you have my attention.

FANS HAVE GOALS

The next thing you need to learn about your fans is what their goals are. Again, if you have no idea, call your favorite clients and ask to interview them. Take them to lunch. Learn about them.

Goals are what drive your customers to actually take action. Sure we all like donuts, but if you have a goal to cut back on sugar, that donut is not really helping you.

When you understand your customer's dreams you can appeal to those goals in your marketing. For instance, my clients' goals are to have a business that allows them to live without struggling to pay the mortgage. Another goal is to be able to spend ample time with their family.

When I create an ad I can say, "Creating a solid business foundation allows you to LAUNCH your business farther without taking time from your family."

> This speaks directly to what my customers actually need instead of constantly talking about myself and what I do.

What are YOUR customers' goals? Do they want to be a better parent? Feel better about themselves? Live a lavish lifestyle? Have the most beautiful yard? Run a business? Graduate from med school? Love themselves no matter what?

What are they reaching for? What are they willing to take action on?

Nobody cares what you do. They don't really care about your business or how you do things. Your customers care about results. They care about what they will get from your program or product or service.

They want to get closer to their objectives. They don't care if you use a "tough-tufted prickly snick-berry switch" to do your job. They don't know what a "tough-tufted prickly snick-berry switch" is. They just care about the results they will get.

If I am going in for a nerve racking surgery, I don't care one iota about the type of scalpel the surgeon has chosen to slice me open with. If he comes into the room telling me all about his equipment, I do not feel better. A monologue about surgical tools doesn't help me feel calm.

What I do care about is a surgeon who tells me what the process looks like for me. What will I need to do? When will I feel better? What assurances can he give me?

The same is true in business. <u>Your potential clients don't care about your equipment or process,</u> ^except that one super nerd^.

> They care about themselves. They care about
> the results.

FANS DISLIKES

Again, think of your business like a planet. You are creating a whole space, another world for your clients. When you do this, you can further ensure your planet attracts the right fans by also understanding your fans' fears and dislikes.

When you know what your fans and potential fans dislike you can eliminate those things from your planet. I don't like rap music. My sister hates country music. I am going to be instantly repelled from a place that has rap music blasting all of the time. My sister is going to be instantly repelled from a place that has country music on all the time.

If you are blasting your fans' dislikes, they are not going to go out of their way to shop with you. They will not go out of their way to explore what you have to offer.

Your mission is to eliminate as many dislikes as you can from your planet.

There is no way to eliminate all of the dislikes for every human on earth. This is part of why we choose a target market. You cannot please everyone. But you can learn about your fans and eliminate all of the common dislikes.

If you deal mostly with very sensitive and kind-hearted Christian people, you probably want to make sure your business avoids cuss words.

Let's say you own a luxury spa. Your fans are millennials without kids. They like 90's music, silence (hence the reason they have no kids), and Harry Potter. Their goals are to have high powered careers and make $200k annually.

Let's say that you, u*nlike your spa's target market,* do have kids. Most of your team have kids as well. You set up a little daycare/play area in the waiting room to help you and your team with childcare. The TV and sound system have cartoons and modern kids music. Your team really likes it because you are family friendly.

Your spa is rapidly losing customers. Very few people make return appointments. Most clients seem a little irritated when they leave and you can't figure out what the issue is. Your services are fantastic. You only use the highest quality items. Your team is dedicated and well qualified.

Why are clients not returning?

Clients are not returning to your imaginary luxury spa because you are not providing the right experience. You know what your fans like and what their goals are. But instead of creating a planet just for them you tried to merge two different planets (yours and theirs).

They don't want to listen to kids' music. They don't want to have to interact with your kids in the waiting room. They don't care about kids cartoons. What should have been a great experience for them was tainted with all of the other things you added.

Your brand did not match your fans so your fans didn't stick around.

The fans (or potential fans) are childless. They don't have to deal with kids on a regular basis so filling a waiting room with them is not going to bring your fans flocking to your door. It will probably send them running.

I will leave a restaurant if the music is so loud, I cannot hear the people I went out with. That is a huge dislike for me. I am old. I have kids, there is already too much noise in my life.

As a business owner, part of your job is to preserve your planet. You keep the dislikes out and the likes in. That means, if you run a restaurant catering to business people who like to have lunch meetings, you are going to keep the place mostly quiet and calm. If someone asks you to turn the music way up, your staff should already know the answer is no. They are preserving the culture of your planet.

Your business should be built to provide your clients with an experience they will return for again and again and again. You can only create an experience your fans crave when you understand what your fans like and what they dislike.

FEAR YOUR FANS HARBOR

You need to know about your fans' fears. Your fans' fears are things like, "What if I am fat forever." "What if my kids grow up to hate me?" "What if I am made fun of for my junky car?" "I listen to too many true crime podcasts and now I get in my car alone at night."

These are the things they worry about, the concerns they have when they go to sleep. These are the issues in their life that plague them. This is probably not, "I really hate spiders." We want to think a little bit deeper. (Unless you own a pest control company. Then you dig into that hatred of spiders.)

Your planet should help alleviate some of your clients' fears. You should be avoiding things that would trigger them.

Let's go back to the example of the luxury spa.

We will pretend these childless and single women are afraid they are going to die alone. Your objective as a business is to not bring that up everytime they come in *(fun fact: single women without kids are ranked as the happiest sub-set of human beings (Reed). So I am not suggesting single, childless women are actually afraid of anything.)*

When your clients come in you are not going to ask them when they are getting married. You don't talk about your kids. You don't tell them about some widow who died and no one found her for three days.

Know your audience. Know your target market.

You need to work your knowledge of your fans' fears into the culture inside your business.

Frequently, you can help to alleviate fears. Perhaps this is the purpose of your business. This would be true if your business taught self defense. In that case, you would be open and loud about the fears of your clients. They are afraid they could be attacked. You help them solve that fear.

In order to create the kind of experience your fans will line up around the block for, you have to understand your fans. Once you realize what your fans like and dislike, your choices get a lot easier.

No, you cannot turn the music all the way up.

No, you cannot bring your child to work.

No, you cannot play your random playlist.

No, we don't use language like that.

Yes, we always say, "My pleasure."

Yes, nerd culture references are always welcome.

When you know what you are aiming for, everything on your planet becomes very carefully curated to attract your fans, protect your fans, and keep everyone else moving along. You want your fans to enjoy working with you.

> You want your ideal client to ache to visit your business again and again.

KNOW, LIKE, AND TRUST – BUT WITH A PLAN

We buy from people we know, like, and trust. This is not new information.

When you hear "know, like, and trust" you probably think of family and friends. Your friends know you, like you, and probably trust you. Yet, the reality of business is that your raving fans will probably not be your family and friends.

Your family and friends know you in a different way. My family and friends know me as loud, emotional, fun, and opinionated Kara. They have probably seen me lose my temper far too many times. They grew up with me. They know my weaknesses and for some of them, they still see me as a twelve-year-old kid. I wouldn't hire that twelve-year-old to teach me about business either.

As you build a rapport with potential fans, you give them the opportunity to know you as an expert in your field. You want to build enough of a relationship that they like you, not as a best buddy, but as an expert in your field. They want to learn from you, work with you, chat with you.

Many of us have been taught the "know, like, and trust" theory. Here's the part you probably weren't taught. The trust piece isn't "I trust this person not to rob me."

The trust piece is trusting someone to do the job. I trust this contractor to finish my garage and make it safe. You trust me to teach you about business. I trust my grocery store to always have too high of prices and rip us all off -- oh, see? I clearly don't trust my grocery store to do what is best for me.

I trust an Uber driver to not kidnap me and murder me in the woods (most of the time). I trust Spaghetti Tree Puzzles to make the most adorable puzzles.

Building trust with your potential customers isn't proving you are a stand up fellow. This trust isn't, "will you watch my bag" trust. This trust is, do I trust them to give me the results I need? Afterall, I trust my neighbor a lot. I even know him and like him. But, I do NOT trust him to perform surgery.

Prove you are an expert in your field.

One of the best ways to build this trust is to offer something of value to your customer that also highlights your expertise. This trust builder is usually a free offer. This can be a car buying guide, a hands on art therapy class, a checklist on how to create a solid business foundation, the first chapter of your book, a free sample, a movie trailer. The list goes on and on.

Once you come in contact with your potential clients, ask them all the questions, and start to create a connection (this is the "know and like" piece). You need to offer them your proof in some way.

What does proof look like for your business?

Give potential fans the opportunity to trust you.

I can love you to death and trust you to tend my kids, but it doesn't mean I trust you to cut my hair or wax my eyebrows. A few of my friends have made that mistake and let me wax their eyebrows. One went nearly eyebrow-less for a month.

I can know you and like you a lot but not trust you to take me rappelling or skydiving.

Building trust is teaching your potential customers you can deliver what you promise. This means you need to be able to show your results.

This is the start of your customer journey.

BE AN ATTENTION GRABBER

What is a customer journey?

A customer journey is the steps your customers take to go from, "Hey. I just met you," to "Here's my number. Call me, maybe," to "Here's my money."

Customer journeys start with grabbing your potential fans' attention, building a relationship (know, like, and trust) then asking for a sale. This is a step-by-step process we need to take every client through. Let's take it from the top.

We are highly distractible creatures. Getting your fans' attention may not be easy.

Due to the ease by which we jump topics, ads, and videos you need a fast attention grabber to lead out your customer journey. This world of overwhelming distraction is another huge reason to know who your target market is.

Yesterday, I had a woman walk into my office. The first thing she saw was my giant LEGO Hedwig. She immediately exclaimed, "Oh my gosh!! Look at Hedwig! That is so cool!"

Attention grabbed. I wasted an entire month of my life building a life sized Hedwig just so it can sit in my office. But, it's an attention grabber, so maybe it was worth it.

I was at a Christmas market in Switzerland this last year. As we were walking by a booth my kids noticed a Christmas gnome cutout. They immediately wanted to take pictures with their heads in the hole. They NEEDED to be a part of it.

Attention grabbed.

What can you do to grab the attention of your fans while still staying on brand? Get their attention and get it fast.

If your target was cops you could scream, "FREE DOUGHNUTS!" into a crowd

(my dad was a cop so I can make that joke).

Last year, I was scrolling Facebook and there was a free printable to track the number of books I read in a year. It was also a coloring page. And it was adorable. That is everything I care about. Take all of my contact info, I need that printable.

Attention grabbed.

USE WHAT YOU KNOW

Lucky for you we already covered the likes, goals, dislikes, and fears of your potential fan. Most of your ad is already written. Let me illustrate.

Using the imaginary luxury spa we already talked about, we take one fear from the fear section, three goals from the goal section, and sprinkle in the likes from the likes section to create the following ad copy.

"Have stress that is eating you alive? At The Flourish and Blotts Spa we can help you relax, rejuvenate, and step into that power suit ready to take on the week! Book your appointment with our free app. Our house elves will be ready for you!"

Remember, the luxury spa's ideal clients (or fans) were high powered career women who had a love of Harry Potter. A luxury Harry Potter themed spa? Yeah, they are hitting that up.

If you own an outdoor adventure company who caters to families with small children you can pull from your likes, goals, and fears to create, "Looking for a safe, fun, and affordable family adventure?? Give your littles an experience they will never forget when you book a scenic tour with Blues and Boats Jones. Just sit back, relax, and enjoy the view while we take care of everyone. Noise canceling headphones included for parents."

The fears amongst that group of fans is that their kids won't be safe. They are also afraid of not giving their kids good enough experiences. They dislike the stress of travel. They like adventure, they like family friendly. Their goals are to take their kids on experiences they will always remember. They want to create memories with their kids.

As you start to figure out the introduction piece of your funnel, use what you know about your fans. We already did most of the work. You just have to put it together.

Sometimes we really, really, REALLY want to just post a video on social media, have it go viral, and make one million dollars. 1000% I hope "virality" happens every time I post anything. My social media is a daily disappointment.

The reality is virality doesn't happen for 99% of businesses.

On average your potential customers need to come in contact with your business 7-12 times just to remember who you are. You need ten memorable interactions before your future fan even knows you exist.

This is like dating in high school all over again. I am obsessed with the guy who walks in front of me to class everyday and I have to yell, "HI JAMIE" for ten days before he even knows I exist. True story though. He is my husband now. Poor schmuck.

Getting through your fans' attention filter enough to be remembered is step number one. And honestly, when it comes to marketing, it's a step we forget about a lot. You have to consistently put yourself out there.

BRING DOWN THE BARRIERS!!

Once you have your fans' attention you need to make it EASY to shop with you.

When you are working to move potential fans to hiring you, you have to make it easy. Shopping with you should be simple. Remove as many purchasing barriers as possible.

A purchase barrier is simply an added step between your customer and cash in your hand. Barriers make it harder for people to shop with you. Clicking through to another page is a purchasing barrier. It is a small one but the more clicks you require the less likely clients are to purchase.

Asking people to come into your store is a purchasing barrier, as is charging for shipping, asking clients to get on a call, or only offering a QR code as your only source of additional information.

A huge purchasing barrier is being hard to find online. All of your social media (business and personal) should easily direct others to where and how they can shop with you. *All of it.* I cannot tell you how much time in my life I have wasted trying to figure out how to purchase from small businesses.

Eliminate as many purchasing barriers as you can.

The process of working with your business needs to be clean and clear. There should be no doubt in your clients' mind what comes next. Make sure you are clearly stating what they need to do to take the next step to work with you.

Think of it like a map. How do they get their spaceship to your planet? You don't just tell people your home exists when they are coming to visit you for the first time, you make sure they have a way to get turn-by-turn instructions.

You need to do the same for your business.

These turn-by-turn instructions need to be small steps. You are not going to meet a potential fan then immediately ask them if you can clean their bathroom. ^That is how the cops get called^.

Each step in your customer's journey needs to be a small and obvious next step. Higher commitment is a larger step than a small commitment. Buying an ice cream is a much smaller commitment than buying a freezer.

The more expensive the item, the larger the step. Buying a $5 pair of sunglasses is a much easier step than buying a $500 pair of sunglasses.

Increased vulnerability also makes the next step scarier. Asking our doctor for help with a broken arm is far less vulnerable than asking our doctor to look at the weird growth that has been gaining velocity and size near our lower region.

Remember these things as you are creating the next steps for your clients. The bigger the commitment, the more steps you need to lead up to a purchase.

Easy baby steps can include things like free downloads, short and low cost webinars, booking from apps, ordering online, signing up for a free coupon, etc. Eliminate all the purchasing barriers you can and make each step of your customer journey as easy and painless as possible.

Think of the navigation on your phone. It gives you clear ^most of the time^ instructions for each step of your trip. If you get lost, it re-routes you ^although with an attitude^. You want to do the same for your clients, but without the attitude.

THANK YOU FOR COMING, HERE IS YOUR TREAT

Give them the first step, "Start driving North on Main Street". Then you give them the next step and the next step. Along the way you are building trust, leaving little motivational treats, and creating a relationship so when the time comes to purchase big items your clients are ready.

If you have a high commitment, high cost, or high vulnerability service or product this journey is going to be a lot longer than if you sell burgers. Everyone wants a burger. Even the vegans want a burger or we wouldn't have plant based patties.

As I write this I have a very stubborn two-year-old at my house. He has all the opinions and ^is definitely right about 100% of everything.^

Sometimes he doesn't want his diaper changed. Sometimes he doesn't want to walk up the stairs on his own. Sometimes life is just too hard.

Unbeknownst to me, my nine-year-old trained him to take one step at a time. He will put a piece of popcorn on the stairs. The two-year-old will walk just far enough to get the popcorn. The nine-year-old will plant another popcorn, one step higher. And so the pattern continues until the two-year-old is in the right room and doing what he is supposed to.

Here's the catch though, if the nine-year-old puts the popcorn too far away, the two-year-old will not move. He will spend nearly all of his energy laying on the ground and crying. He is only willing to move forward if the next step is easy.

Your potential customers are the same. Yes, we want to get into shape. Yes, we want a clean house. Yes, we want to be happier, have successful business, and do all the things. It also sounds too hard. We want to take easy steps.

Think of your future fans like my stubborn two-year-old. You have to give them one step at a time, with fun little bonuses, and exciting moments along the way to keep them moving forward.

If you are a restaurant this can look like signing up for a coupon code. That is step one. Step two might be placing a mobile order and using the code. Step three is giving them an amazing experience with your company. And step four is turning them into loyal fans by always giving them a great experience and rewarding them for shopping with you.

A restaurant is easy.

What about an expensive service? What about selling a house?

Step one can look like giving a free "Ten Things You NEED to Know Before Buying a House" to families who are renting. You can distribute those in all kinds of ways. Step two might look like offering a free online assessment of their readiness to buy. Step three could look like inviting them to an open house you are hosting, or seven.

Step four would be having coffee and just talking about what they are looking for in a home. Step five is sending them some home options. Step six might be asking them to set up a meeting time. Step seven is meeting, signing a contract, and officially house hunting together.

See the difference?

Every step is a small, easy, low commitment next step. Keep things simple.

The first steps to creating successful marketing for your business are to understand exactly who you are building your business for. Know, with a doubt, what they like and dislike. Know what their goals and fears are.

The next step is to create a beautiful customer journey that makes shopping with you a breeze and a rewarding experience.

NEXT STEPS

Use your clients likes, goals, fears, and dislikes to create a customer journey optimized for them.

Determine if you need a long or a short journey for your ideal customer experience.

For more help and resources on defining your customer journey, jump into a Launched workshop. Scan this code or head to the website to get any of the bonuses mentioned in this chapter. This will also help keep you updated on our next Launch Your Business Academy.

Scan the code or visit:
launchedacademy.com/book-bonuses

🪐 CHAPTER 8
WHY CAN'T I FIND YOU

"How can online shoppers shop with your business if you aren't giving them the option?"

You already know the internet is a big deal. You use it every day. It is probably how you found this book.

And yet, I constantly have business owners tell me their business doesn't need to be online. Their business is different, their business is custom, their business is local. It does not matter what type of business you have, your business needs to be online.

NASDAQ estimates that 95% of all purchases will be online by 2040. (Djuraskovic) We are already buying cars, food, home decor, coaching, and furniture online. If your business is not there, it will be skipped over.

90% of the US population uses the Internet. Why would you hide from that amount of the population?

Over $7.9 billion in online sales happen on Cyber Monday alone. Are you getting a piece of the pie? Are you taking advantage of the internet or are you hiding from it?

91% of social media users have visited a store because of an online experience. If you are needing more shoppers in your store, being online is a great way to bring those customers into your store. After all, your competition is literally in the palm of their hand. You should be there too.

Even if you are not tech savvy, you can get your business online.

E-COMMERCE

Only 26% of small businesses have tried to create their own online commerce. That means even though 76% of the US population shops online, only a quarter of small businesses are giving the population an opportunity to shop with their business.

How can online shoppers shop with your business if you aren't giving them the option?

And don't give me that, "I'm local" mumbo-jumbo. Being online still matters. Not only can you expand your business online, you can cash in on the convenience factor.

We are all busy. We have 80,000 things to do in a day and sometimes, we just want to pick our groceries up on the curb. It is easier to compare prices, find exactly what you are looking for, and look up reviews while shopping online.

Start making it easier for your fans to shop with you. When COVID took over the planet, the businesses most equipped to survive were the businesses who were set up online.

SOCIAL PROOF

We do not just shop online, we also research online.

Even if we plan on walking into a store to shop, we still do research online. 87% of shoppers today use e-commerce reviews to decide, not only if they like a product, but if they like a business. (Alaimo) Your potential fans are using the internet to determine the trustworthiness of your business.

This is what we call "social proof". When we try to research a company and they don't have any online presence, it does not make us trust them. We don't know anything about that business. How long have they been in business? What do their past projects look like? Do they have any client complaints?

Creating easy ways for potential customers to interact with your business online builds credibility and trust with your business. Potential clients are most likely to shop with you if they can see how you have helped others.

If you are not online, if you are not claiming your online listings, you are abandoning those research opportunities. The only thing people will find are the complaints unhappy customers wrote about you on their blogs.

MAKE THINGS EASY

Being online can also make running your business easier. You *can* literally make money while you are sleeping. Your customers can still shop with you even when your business is not open. They can impulse buy their cute, little hearts out.

Lean into that!

You don't have to be in your shop, you don't have to answer calls and emails. Your customers can book appointments, order from your store, request quotes, and so much more when you are accessible online.

This does not mean just having a social media presence. But we will get more into that in a moment.

EXPAND YOUR MARKET

Moving your business online allows you not only to make money while you sleep but it also allows you to expand your market.

Your business is no longer confined to the town it resides in. You can ship your products all over the world. You can offer your services to places you have never even been before. And if you are thinking, "Oh man, I can't do that, my product/service is different."

> I would bet you $1000 I can come up with a way for you to sell something online that allows you to expand your business and your market reach.

Restaurant? Sell swag, gift cards, or "secret" recipes. Bottle that sauce and sell it!

Construction company? Sell your blueprints, offer easy how-tos, create a mini course on how to hire and manage a contractor.

Gift shop? Are you kidding me? Just put your products online!

And for those of you who are thinking I am crazy because of course people have their business online, you are wrong. I love you but you are wrong. *So many companies* are skipping this step.

🪐 YOUR FIND-ABILITY SCORE

Now that I have convinced you to embrace the internet, I have some bad news.

Putting your business online is not enough.

Just having a website or social media pages is *not* enough. People will not start showing up just because your business is online. The idea of *"build it they will come"* is a very, very outdated marketing idea (think early 1900s).

Yet we all do it.

One of the many things I have done in my life is design websites. I have created websites for large and small companies. One thing my clients had in common was a belief that once their website was online, they would start raking in the cash overnight.

According to Google there are 1.14 billion websites in the world. 1.14 billion. How do fans find you in that hay stack? Once you get online your next job is to make sure you can be found!

This brings us to the findability score. *You can download your findability assessment with the QR code at the end of this chapter.*

I created this assessment to help business owners see and rate how hard they are to find online. *Don't get discouraged.* Every single business on the planet started with a findability score of zero. It is *not* crazy hard to make sure you can be found online. Sure, there are 1.14 billion websites in the world. But you aren't competing with all of them.

You need to make sure you can be found within your industry then your niche. You don't have to be everywhere, you do need to be visible enough that your fans can find you without searching every dark corner of the internet.

Your findability score will give you a solid idea of how well you are ranking and what you can easily do to help your business be found.

GOOGLE BUSINESS LISTING

You can download the Findability Score Worksheet on my website for the whole exciting experience *(see QR code at the end of the chapter)*.

If you are not ready for that level of commitment ^I know it's a lot to ask^, I will just walk you through the basics.

The first thing you need to do to get your business visible is to make sure you have a Google My Business listing (aka Google Business Profile). This is a free business listing. It helps Google know if your business is legit or not.

Go set it up. You simply go to google.com/business and follow the prompts. When your Google Business Listing is set up and verified, you will get this cool little feature where your business shows up in Google listings.

It is free. It tells people how to shop with you. It is free. You make money.

Go set it up. Right now.

Put the book down and go take care of this. Today. Seriously. Stop reading. And if you are driving and you are listening to this, you best get it done when you get home. Before you make the excuse, yes, you can have a Google Business Listing even if your business is in your home. And, no, you do not have to make your address public.

THE GOOGLE CHECKLIST

SEO (search engine optimization) is what we use to basically say, "How much does Google really care about you? Are you on page one?". SEO is a long game. You are not going to set up your business website and have it ranking on the first page of Google by the next day.

This is part of why a Google Business listing is so important. You don't have to play the SEO game quite as much with a business listing.

We are not going to cover all of the things you can do to battle your way to the top of the search results. Like I said, it is a long game. But, we can give you the basics to make sure your website shows up when people Google your business name and location.

It is really easy, are you ready? Make sure ALL THE WORDS are on your website.

If you are a restaurant in Springville, SD you are going to use the phrase, "restaurant in Springville, SD" throughout your website. If you sell handmade Navajo pottery, you are going to use that phrase throughout your entire website.

Make sure you have images, make sure you have at least 300 words on each page. Do the basics to get started. You don't have to overthink this.

Here is a really quick hack to see if you have your search terms on your website. Simply go to Google. In the search bar type, site:yourbusiness.com + your search term.

If your business is Launched you will type: site:launchedacademy.com "business education in Utah". If your business is Bear Skins Custom Ink and you are located in Blanding, UT you will type: site:bearskinscustomink.com "Custom t-shirts in Blanding UT"

This will force Google to search only your website for your selected phrase. In less than a second you will know exactly how many times your phrase comes up on your website, or how many times it doesn't.

Your first step to make sure your website is ranking on Google, is to make sure your search terms are actually included within your website.

I CAN'T FIND YOU ON SOCIAL

You know when you are on social and you see something you really like? You feel like you need it right now! You ask about it and the person says something like, "Yeah, I make these in my business."

You are 100% ready to buy, but when you ask for more info they just give you their store name. You Google their store name, you can't find their store anywhere on the internet. They don't have a link on their profile and you can't find their page on any social platforms.

Don't be this business.

I cannot tell you how many hours of my life I have wasted trying to track down a business online. Your personal social media needs to direct people to your business accounts. It's okay if your friends and family know you run a business!

> Make sure everyone can easily, EASILY find your business from your personal social pages. It should be in your bio. With a link.

I will die on this hill.

People are trying to shop with you and you are making it impossibly hard. Go, right now, and make sure your business is listed on all your personal profiles. I can wait.

🪐 YOUR WEBSITE & GOOGLE

You need to do more for your online presence than just post on social media.

Social media platforms are a wonderful ^and definitely not a completely soul sucking^ way to get your business out to the masses. But, they are not a website and should not be a replacement for a website.

While social media is vital for your business it is also chaos. There are one million ways for your fans to get distracted. Your content is different everyday. Finding the one item you were looking for on social media is a crap shoot at best and dumpster fire most of the time.

We have to sort through so much content just to find what we are looking for.

When your potential customers visit your social media page how do they know immediately how to shop with you? How many scrolls before they find the post about signing up for your workshop? How many scrolls until they find the coupon you have been advertising?

A website takes all the information and consolidates it into one space, where there is nothing to distract anyone. On a good website everything is easy to find, and your fans know what to do next.

Your website can also rank on Google over and over again. Each page is another opportunity to be found by more and more fans. Your social media pages can only be ranked only.

The purpose of your website is to help your friends and fans spend money. You want people to be able to book appointments, learn what you offer, see why you are an expert, and most importantly *spend money.*

Let's be really honest with each other. We want money. WE WANT THE MONEY! I want the money. You want the money. We all need money. Let's make it easy for people to give us the money.

Investing in a website is vital.

COMMON WEBSITE MISTAKES

A website should be a sales page, it should help people feel confident in spending money with you. A website is a great place to build trust.

Make sure you avoid these mistakes:

Poor image quality. You are selling stuff here; have great images. With all the free stock photos available there are no more excuses.

Long blocks of text. We are scanners, we scan websites, not read every word.

WHY CAN'T I FIND YOU

Kind of how you scanned the headlines in this book before you started reading it. One, long block of text isn't scannable and people will leave quickly. Break everything up so it is easy to consume.

Only one page. The single page websites have increased in popularity over the years. However, they kill your SEO because your website can only be ranked once. They are also overwhelming to potential customers because once again they have to scroll and scroll to find what they are looking for.

WEBSITE MUST HAVES

On the other hand there are some things you should make sure your website has. For every "do not" there is a "do".

A call to action. A call to action is a "next step" for your clients. It tells them what to do if they are interested in what you are selling. This can be "Book Now!", "Start Shopping", or "Change Your Life". It needs to be clear. It needs to be clickable.

A way to collect leads. Every website should have a way to gather contact information. This needs to be more than "sign up for our newsletter". Remember when we talked about the customer journey and what you can offer in exchange for contact info? This is that moment.

What is the baby step on your website to get your fans interested? A free e-book? 50 email subject lines that get opened? Free breadsticks? Mmm, breadsticks.

Contact info. Please, for everything that is glorious and nerdy in the world, be sure to have your contact info on your website. This includes a phone number, an email address, and at the very least the city where your business resides.

A contact form is not enough.

Testimonials. Make sure your website has reviews from your current fans. Lots and lots of reviews. Use real names! Use photos!

Don't have any reviews yet? Go ask for them!!

Your Clear Next Step. The single, most important thing your business website needs is a very clear next step. This can be your call to action (book now) or a sign up form for your opt in. But you need to make sure your customers know what they need to do next to work with you.

Outline what the journey with you looks like. Keep it simple, 1-5 steps max. Make sure you are focusing on your customer and their needs, not you and what makes you great.

We don't care how your machine works, we want to know what it is going to do for us. Make sure your customers know what the next step is and why they would take it.

😐 PURCHASING BARRIERS

Sometimes we have traffic to our site. We can be found on Google. We are doing good things but no one seems to be buying. This is where we check out website purchasing barriers.

Putting things in the way of people shopping with us is a purchasing barrier.

CONFUSING WEBSITE

Having a confusing website is a massive barrier to sales. Overall your website and customer journey need to be simple and streamlined.

You know how your grocery store re-arranges things every couple of years? You are left to fumble and try to figure it out on your own. You don't know the next steps. You feel like an idiot. And you are frustrated with the dumbos that put the eggs by the cheese when they used to be by the milk!

We do this to our clients all the time. We get them interested and mildly comfortable thenThey move the eggs, leaving them lost and confused. They have no idea where they are or what they should be doing. And so they bail.

When potential fans arrive on your website they need to be gently walked through their customer journey. Eliminate useless clicking and complicated navigation. We just want to find the freaking eggs!

SHIPPING

48% of shoppers will abandon their carts due to extra costs, such as shipping. (Hotjar) Most people would rather pay for another item than to have to pay shipping.

Remove the shipping barrier from your website. Offer free ground shipping or 5-10 day shipping. Up your prices to cover shipping. Give your clients a way to earn free shipping. Offer free shipping if your customers spend a certain amount of money. At what price point are you willing to pay for shipping yourself?

Find an option that works for you and is financially feasible.

Additional fees are the number one reason shoppers abandon carts. Don't ignore this.

TOO HARD

Another major purchasing barrier is making things too hard. I feel like we have covered this over and over again. I am going to say it again because it is monumentally important.

Shopping with your company is too hard if:

Clients have to spend more than 15 seconds to find a specific item

There are glitches in your shopping cart

Your website doesn't save shopping cart data

There are too many options

The checkout process takes forever

Your website asks too many questions or the same questions over and over

Sit down with a friend who isn't familiar with your website and do some trial runs. How long does it take them to find your itty, bitty, teeny-weeny, yellow polka dot bikinis? How long does the cart store information? How complicated is the checkout process?

Keep it simple. Keep it easy.

PAYMENT PROBLEMS

People often abandon carts because a website does not take their preferred payment method. This does not apply exclusively to online purchases. Around one tenth of customers will abandon carts or shop somewhere else if their current store doesn't offer their preferred payment method.

You don't want to deal with PayPal? 75% of people in the US use PayPal. (Sekulic) You don't want to take credit cards because of the fees? Suck it up, buttercup. Only 9% of people in the US prefer to shop with cash. (Pokora and Perkins)

Paying 3% on credit card fees is worth the price of a sale. Oftentimes it is 3% or no sale.

There used to be a restaurant where I live that hated credit cards. Hated taking cards of every kind. When they first opened they gave discounts for paying in cash. Whoo-hoo! I was thrilled to take that deal.

However, they didn't raise their prices to cover the credit card fees or the cash discount. 3-6% makes a huge difference. By the end of their second year in business they were bitter. They were mad if anyone used a card and started charging a fee to use a card in their store.

They also acted hella annoyed when you pulled out a card.

I was a *dedicated* customer when they first opened. If I wasn't there for breakfast, I was there for lunch. It was right down the street from my office. It was fast. It was good. It was decently healthy. I was happily there all of the time. Yay food!

At first, I was happy and excited to bring cash in. I got rewarded for it.

By the end of the second year, when they started charging fees for using a card, I felt punished. I felt like I was in trouble for shopping with them. There were many times when I realized I didn't have cash and rather than deal with the added fees for "not being prepared" I skipped stopping all together.

Accept your clients payment methods and do it with a smile.

Adjust your prices to cover any expenses. And get a better credit card processing company who takes the fees out before depositing into your account. Shop credit card processing companies for the best rates.

BARRIERS WITH A PURPOSE

Putting things in the way of people giving us money is a purchasing barrier. Occasionally, it makes sense to create intentional purchasing barriers. For instance, the $10 for attending my workshops is a barrier. You have to find your card, put in the numbers, *spend* $10.

I could make them free. That would eliminate a barrier. Obviously, I don't make much money when they are $10.

However, $10 creates a barrier that makes people work for it - just a little bit. They have to decide they want to be there. They have to commit to coming or losing their $10. They have made the decision to invest $10 into their business.

I like this purchasing barrier. I don't have 80% no-shows. I get attendees who are more engaged. I get attendees that want to be a part of what I have to offer. This is a good barrier because it eliminates people in my workshop who don't really care. It eliminates window shoppers.

Part of what makes it a good barrier is that it is intentional and I know how my potential fans are reacting to it.

I can also remove it if it stops giving me the results I want.

My application for my Launch Your Business Academy also has some barriers. I don't take everyone who applies into my program. I am very selective. The application process reflects this standard. It is a long application, people have to have some commitment to get through it.

If you are having client issues in your business. Perhaps you are attracting too many foes. A barrier of some kind can help ease the issue.

🪐 USING SOCIAL MEDIA

Social Media has become a huge part of running a business. It's time to learn the basics.

What is the purpose of social media in your business?

This is not a trick question and there is no "right" answer. The purpose is going to be different for every business. Finding your purpose is the first thing you need to accomplish when starting, or growing, your social media pages.

Is your purpose on social media to go viral and have more sales than you can keep up with? Are you looking to be famous? Are you just wanting a general presence so people can find you?

Do you want a lot of followers? Do you want to make money? How are you making money? Do you need a platform so you can run ads and drive people to your website? Are you educating your potential clients? Are you looking for lead collection?

When you understand your purpose for being online, you can make better choices. If you don't know what end game you are looking for online, you are just aimlessly spending time.

So write it out. Why do you want your business to be on social media? What is your purpose?

DON'T WASTE YOUR TIME

We all know social media can be a *huge* waste of time. Especially if you are the type, like me, to get incredibly distracted and accidently spend an hour scrolling when you were just trying to track down an email.

Make sure your time on social media aligns with your social media mission.

> Stop scrolling and start using the platforms to
> your advantage.

If you are just on social media so people can find you if they search directly for you, you don't need to spend a lot of time on the apps. You don't have to have a huge social media following in order to have a successful business. You just need the basics so potential clients can find you.

Have a purpose to your social media posting and interacting. Manage your time like any other job, clocking in and clocking out. If you are constantly checking and checking social media it will eat all of your time and energy.

WHERE ARE YOUR FANS?

We have talked a lot about fans, the people who shop with you, love your business and keep you moving forward. Your business needs to be on social platforms to be where your fans are.

Take some time and do your research. Ask your fans what social apps they are using. Look at the stats. Then choose the app(s) where they hang out the most. If your fans are not on a certain app, feel free to skip that one.

Use your time and resources well by going where your fans already are. Find those watering holes! If you are just starting and you don't have any social platforms yet, choose the one with the highest concentration of your fans.

Start there.

CONTENT PILLARS

Your business social accounts are not for all the little things in your life. No one cares that you made your own human. We agree he is cute, but we don't care that you made him. I made three humans. They are the living embodiments of my impulsive decisions, constantly following me around asking for snacks.

No one cares about my small humans.

> We love you, but unless your human, dog, cat, turtle, or porcupine is modeling the clay earrings you make and sell, your audience doesn't care.

Instead choose 3-5 five content pillars. These pillars are the core topics that you talk about on your social platforms. These should all align with your brand, one of them should be sales.

If you are a nail salon your pillars might be: Nail care, beautiful nail designs, book with us, nail problems, and about our team.

If your business is a construction company your pillars might be: Look what we built!!, construction 101, what to ask your contractor, get a quote, and hilarious construction fails.

My content pillars are: business tips and hacks, Launched promos, entrepreneur humor, client highlights and reviews, and entrepreneur motivation.

Having content pillars helps you curate consistency on your platforms. We learned in chapter three that consistency is what allows our clients to remember us. You need to be consistent if you are going to break through those mental filters.

YOUR SOCIAL STRATEGY

Figure out which platforms you should be on, how to maximize your time, and then identify your content pillars. After that, you need to map out your social media strategy.

How are you delivering those content pillars? How does the delivery of our content pillars change based on the social media platforms you are using?

If you really want to see strong success on social media, you need to have a plan and a strategy. You are not going to post content, just to post content. You should not be flooding the internet with as much content as you can.

You need a plan, a strategy that is directly related to your social media endgame. We could go really deep into this and take up another chapter, but I just want you to get started. Here are the basics.

You are going to sit down and determine three things:

ONE: What metrics you are going to track on your social platforms (likes, follow, engagement, sales, etc)

TWO: What types of posts you will be creating for each platform. Article based content, photo heavy content, video led content, or something else all together. You can create themed days, like Business Tip Tuesday!

THREE: How you will track your progress. Posting and posting and posting is not going to get you anywhere if you have no idea what is working. Create a way to track which posts are the most effective and which ones are duds.

This will give you the ability to curate more content that your followers would like to see. More importantly, tracking allows you to see what type of content brings you closer to your social media goals.

Do not forget that having a million followers may not be your goal and that is okay. Twenty four followers that shop with you are worth more than one million who don't. Quality of quantity.

Download the template for your social media strategy using the QR code at the end of this chapter for a step-by-step guide.

GOING VIRAL

Here's a harsh reality. Your business will probably not go viral.

Yes, some businesses go viral and a few even find wild success there. That is not the norm. Social media platforms want you to think that is the norm so you continue to try, you continue to play the social media lottery. They strategically push out content of creators showing their viral success. It is not an accident that you see those videos so often, it's a strategy to keep you engaged.

The reality is the 1,700,000 pieces of content are uploaded to Facebook alone every MINUTE. Every minute. If one new piece of content goes viral every minute ^and we all know that isn't happening^ you would still have less than a one in 1.7 million chance of going viral.

This is why we have a purpose and our own strategy for social media. Hoping to go viral is great, but like playing the lottery, is not a guaranteed pay out. It is a hope you have no control of.

Focus on what you can control.

Create a plan. Be consistent.

NEXT STEPS

Do an audit on your online presence. Know where you sit, and how hard you are to find, so that you know what to work on next. Don't forget to download the Findability Worksheet of the Social Media Strategy template.

For more help and resources to improve your online presence, jump into a Launched workshop. Scan this code or head to the website to get any of the bonuses mentioned in this chapter. This will also help keep you updated on our next Launch Your Business Academy.

Scan the code or visit:
launchedacademy.com/book-bonuses

🪐 SECTION THREE
THE RACE TO PROFITABILITY

CHAPTER 9

FINANCE THAT FINALLY MAKES SENSE

"You are worth investing in. Your business is worth investing in."

Oftentimes as business owners, we avoid the finances. They can feel overwhelming and confusing. We are afraid of what they might tell us so we solidly avoid them and hope for the best.

I hope this chapter gives you a little more financial confidence. Your finances, after all, are telling you really important things about your business. If you are not paying attention, you can't make good financial decisions.

🪐 PERSONAL FINANCE VS BUSINESS FINANCE

Let's get started with the difference between personal finance and business finance. Personal finance and business finance are not the same.

When I first heard this I thought, "Duh, because you have to track your business finance for taxes."

Oh boy. Yes, *but*, there is so much more. You should not be managing your business finances the same way you manage personal finances.

I am going to teach this to you the exact same way my first business mentor taught it to me. Imagine you want to buy a boat. It is a $5,000 boat and you don't have the money for it. So, you take out a loan at 29% interest. It is not a good deal. You drive the boat a few times and end up paying significantly more than it's worth in interest.

Most people will agree that it's a bad financial decision.

Now, imagine you bought that same boat, but as a business investment -- meaning, you want to make more money with the boat.

You still don't have the money for the boat so you get a 29% interest loan for it. Then you take it to the lake and you rent it out for $400/day for four days a week. $400/day is a good price for a boat. Four days a week is only a 57% booking rate.

At the end of twelve weeks you will have $19,200. On a $5,000 investment.

Not only can you pay off the boat and all of the interest but you are up over $14,000. Fourteen thousand dollars. Buy a second boat to rent out and you are up $28,000. Increase your daily rental by $150 and you are up over $33,000.

That is a good business decision. That boat was worth the money and worth the loan it took to purchase it.

> Business finance decisions are not made on emotions with personal finance guidelines. Business finance decisions are made on spreadsheets with return on investment guidelines and proof of concept.

Don't go out and buy five boats because I told you a story. Do the research, do the work and know what your investment can bring you. We didn't start with five boats. We started with one, to prove our theory. *Then* we go out and invest in more boats. After we prove the concept we begin to grow our investment.

Do not run your business like you run your personal life. Money is not scary. Money is a tool. Learn how to use it to multiply what you already have.

I wrote this book with women in mind. In general, most male business owners I come in contact with do not have a hard time investing in their business or themselves. They paid well for their education, for their equipment, and typically aren't too afraid of paying for advertising.

If you have a hard time justifying why you should spend money on your business and on your education, listen up.

You are depriving yourself, your future clients, and your family of all the incredible things you bring to the world when you hide behind a fear of finances. You are just as worth investing in as anyone else. You don't need permission to invest in yourself and your business. You know you are capable of amazing things -- go out and get them!

You are worth investing in. Your business is worth investing in.

🪐 FINANCE VOCABULARY – WHAT IN THE WORLD ARE YOU SAYING?

Before we move ahead, I want to make sure we all understand a few finance/

accounting words correctly. Or that we are at least on the same page.

When you take business classes or go to business conferences, it can feel like everyone knows things you don't. They flash around vocab no one explained to you. ^Or, maybe I was asleep or talking to a friend when they tried to teach me.^

So here the finance vocab words that are most commonly misunderstood:

- **Revenue:** The total amount of money that came into your business from sales. Nothing taken out. All of the money.

- **Cost of Goods Sold**: The cost of the things you sell. If you sell t-shirts, how much did the shirt cost? How much did you pay to get the shirt designed and printed? That is Cost of Goods Sold or COGS.

- **Gross Profit:** The total amount of money that came into your business minus the cost of goods sold.

- **Profit**: Often called net profit, this is the total amount you made after all your costs are subtracted from your revenue. Plot twist, some business owners include what they paid themselves in this and some do not. Always ask if you have questions.

- **Assets**: Anything you own in your business. This includes money, your website, equipment, and inventory.

- **Liabilities**: Any claims anyone has to assets in your business. If you bought a business computer with a loan, the computer is an asset, the loan is a liability.

PRICING YOUR PRODUCTS

Throw everything you have ever heard about pricing out the window. 90% of the advice you were ever given is trash advice.

Your dad's, brother's, best-friend's business partner told you to just double all your costs? He is wrong.

Your Great Aunt Sally told you to triple your costs (a third for profit, a third for costs, and a third for overhead). She is also wrong. Delete that information from your brain.

Your college professor told you "since you are starting out" you need to look at your competition and price just under them. BOO!

That class you took, with all your industry competition, told you to triple your prices because you don't want to be a commodity you want to be exclusive. Wrong. Everyone is wrong.

There is only *one* way to price your goods and services correctly. And that way is to know your numbers.

> Know your costs and create a pricing strategy to support your business.

Let me explain.

Do not quit on me. I know I just attacked everyone you ever loved, but stick with me. You can still love them and also not take business advice from them.

FIXED COSTS

The first step to pricing your products and services correctly is to figure out your fixed and variable costs.

I heard a funny story once about two men who were selling watermelons. They took their truck to a farm, filled the bed with $1 watermelons then took them to a stand on the side of the road - where they sold the watermelons for $1 each.

Weeks went by and they weren't making any money. ^I know, we are all shocked ^. So – they bought a bigger truck.

Of course we all know that is ridiculous, but I see similar situations happen all the time. Business owners do not know how much they need to make to break even, let alone to actually make money.

> So they make up their prices and can never
> get ahead.

You need to know your fixed costs. Your fixed costs are everything you have to pay for even if you don't make any money. For most business owners this includes: rent, utilities, employees, website expenses, phones, online subscriptions, etc.

You need to know exactly what your fixed costs are each month.

VARIABLE COSTS

Once you know your fixed costs, what it costs you just to keep the lights on, you need to get familiar with your variable costs.

When you make a sale (YAY MONEY!!) you have costs. If you sell a t-shirt, you also have to *buy* the t-shirt. If you sell a custom work of art, you have to make the art. If you sell out all your inventory you have to buy more inventory.

In the Launch Your Business Academy I have a really cool calculator that helps you determine and understand your variable costs. These will obviously be different for each business and sometimes they can feel a little complicated.

We are going to try and simplify it as much as possible. Choose your most popular product. Let's say it is french fries. Next you are going to write down everything you have to buy just to sell said french fries.

It should look something like this:

- Potatoes (6 oz)
- Fry sauce (4 oz) - *yay Utah!*
- Fry sauce container
- Fry basket
- Basket liner
- Napkins (3)
- One sack
- Taxes
- Credit card fees
- Eco friendly fork

There were more items than you thought, weren't there? Or have you priced out a restaurant before?

Next, you are going to go through and figure out how much each of these items costs you. Say you buy 300 napkins for $100. Those three napkins cost you $.03. A bag of potatoes for $.39. Those six ounces cost you $.45.

Follow it all the way through. Know how much your products and services cost you. Do not guess.

Potatoes (6 oz)	$0.39
Fry sauce (4 oz) - *yay Utah!*	$0.21
Fry sauce container	$0.29
Fry basket	$0.41
Basket liner	$0.18
Napkins (3)	$0.03
One sack	$0.15
Taxes	$0.50
Credit card fees	$0.07
Eco friendly fork	$0.06

NOW YOU PRICE!

Once you have those two things: your fixed costs and your variable costs you can begin to figure out your pricing.

Pricing calculations are one of my very favorite business projects. Numbers are fun! Notice the lack of a sarcastrophe. Numbers really are fun. Numbers tell you how to make money. We all started businesses to make money. This is how you do that!

Let's say your fixed costs to run your restaurant is $2000 per month. Those costs include utilities, staff, rent, software, etc. $2000, it is a really low-cost restaurant. Maybe it's a food truck that only sells french fries.

Yes, we are rolling with that.

We will call it the Fat Fry Mobile. It costs the Fat Fry Mobile $2000 per month to cover their fixed costs. Each order of fries cost them $2.25. If they price their fries at $4 they make $1.75 per order.

In order to cover their fixed costs they need to sell 1142 orders of fries each month. Fat Freddie and Thin Thea are only open on the weekends. But not on Sunday because they like Jesus and God and go to church instead. So basically, they are only open on Friday evenings and Saturdays. They need to sell 142 orders of fries each day they're open just to pay their expenses.

MAKE SMART ADJUSTMENTS

Fat Freddie and Thin Thea can now look at this calculation and say, "We can totally kill that. We sell 142 orders of fries without breaking a sweat!". Cool! That might be a great price point for them.

Let's pretend this is out of Fat Freddie and Thin Thea's wheel house. They see 142 orders a day and know it is impossible for them to keep up. Fat Freddie starts to cry.

This is how many business owners look at their numbers. "I can't compete. I can't make money. I can't do this."

But not you! You know *ALL* of your costs. This means you can adjust your prices without sacrificing profit. If we go back and look at your variable costs, your costs include an eco-friendly fork. That fork is a $.50 fork. Let's face it, most people eat fries with their fingers, get rid of the fork. Fat Freddie and Thin Thea choose to get rid of the paper sack as well. Most people immediately throw it away. That saves them another $.15.

Their profit went from $1.75 to $2.40.

Just like that we are down to 833 orders of fries a month or 104 orders per day. *Plus*, they can create a fry sauce up sale. An up sale can add additional income to help make up more of the difference between where they are and where they want to be. They can keep their fries at $4 then charge another $.25 for their ever amazing and exclusive fry sauce.

Now their profit is $2.65 and they only need to sell 94 orders per day!

They *know* they are making money, even if they have to make some adjustments. This is the power of knowing your numbers. If you really know everything that goes into your business, you don't have to panic about pricing and numbers. You simply make the correct adjustments.

PAY. YOUR. FREAKIN'. SELF.

Some of you may have noticed we have left out something very important. When and how do you pay yourself? If Fat Freddie and Thin Thea are selling approx 100 fry orders per day they are bringing in a revenue of $2,120. After they pay their fixed and variable costs they only have $120 left over.

Nobody can live on $120 per month.

What do they do? When do Fat Freddie and Thin Thea start paying themselves?

We just got them profitable! It's only $120 but they are profitable! Now what?

I always encourage business owners to include paying themselves as a fixed cost. I know exactly what my family needs to survive every month.

> Providing for my family is a fixed cost for my business.

When I calculate my prices, putting food on the table is always included.

The added expense of Fat Freddie and Thin Thea needing to pay themselves changes everything. If their family only needs $2000 per month they need to double their profits. Doubling their profits is the only way to make their business financially worth it.

This is where you get to explore unique pricing strategies in your business. If your business is only bringing your family $120 each month we need to have a hard conversation. With Fat Freddie and Thin Thea the solution might be simple. Open their fry truck every evening (except Sunday of course, they still love Jesus). Opening their fry truck five days a week instead of two would give them $10,000 of revenue every month.

Their gross profit (revenue minus cost of goods sold) would be $6,360. Their net profit would be $4,360. If they only needed $2,000/mo to survive, they are going to be okay.

With your business you need to figure out your solutions. Perhaps it looks like reducing more costs, increasing sales, adding upsells, increasing prices, etc. The possibilities are endless.

But you need to start by doing the math.

🪐 A PRICING STRATEGY

I think that some of the issues new business owners have with pricing their products and services is that they are looking for a solid "right" number. They want a book or a class that says, "You should be charging exactly this. If you charge exactly this specific number for your specific service, you will make oodles of money."

A pricing formula like that doesn't exist.

The formula doesn't exist because there are too many variables at play. Each business has different expenses. Business owners have different financial needs. Businesses have different brands. Customers are willing to pay more for luxury or higher-end brands – even if the product is exactly the same.

When pricing goods and services for your company, you are not looking for the "magic number." Instead, create a pricing strategy that fully supports your business at every business stage.

There are so many fun and creative ways to create the pricing strategy that works for you. Selling fry sauce as an up sale instead of in the basket, even though the Fat Fry Mobile is selling it for under their cost (did you notice that), is a pricing strategy.

This strategy allows them to make just a little bit more to help offset their expenses.

Some businesses use a "good, better, best" pricing strategy. This strategy helps push consumers to the item or package that helps the business make the most money.

Setting up pricing for your business is not just about slapping a price tag on everything. You want to create an entire strategy that supports longevity in your business.

COMPETITION AND PRICING

Even though we know our costs, we still need to be aware of our competition and what they are charging. Maybe Fat Freddie looks at his costs and says, "We can't sell fries for $4/ea. The Fast Fry Wagon sells for $2.50. And they park right next to us!!" A lot of business owners are going to see that and think they have to immediately drop their price.

If you drop your price you now have new totals. Instead of needing to sell 90-100 orders of fries each day Fat Freddie and Thin Thea would need to sell 1000 orders of fries each day! That is 100 orders an hour, they would have to be putting out a new order every 90 seconds. And remember they are only open half days on Fridays so it would be every 45 seconds on Friday.

Next, we have the fry sauce and the fry sauce cup. If you are a Utahn you already know fry sauce is typically store made and it is full of mayo. Mayo is expensive, and the serving containers are even more expensive. So we offer ketchup instead and add the fry sauce as an add on. That saves Freddie and Thea another $.50 and they are down to a variable cost of $1.1 per fry.

If Thea and Freddie choose to match their competition's prices they are making a gross profit of $1.40 per fry. They were making $2.65! They are cutting their profit almost in half by getting scared of their competition prices.

The Fat Fry Mobile can definitely choose to lower their prices to match their competition's. They can do what a lot of business owners do and choose to price under their competition.

However, The Fat Fry Mobile knows their numbers now. Because they know their numbers they know they cannot survive on charging $1.40 per fry. The strategy of pricing just under, or just at, their competition will not work for them.

Like The Fat Fry Mobile

> you have to cultivate a strategy that will fully support
> your business, not slightly delay your bankruptcy.

THE PRICING BELL CURVE

Most of life runs on a bell curve. This is a bell curve about fry costs. Your industry pricing is the same, it has a bell curve.

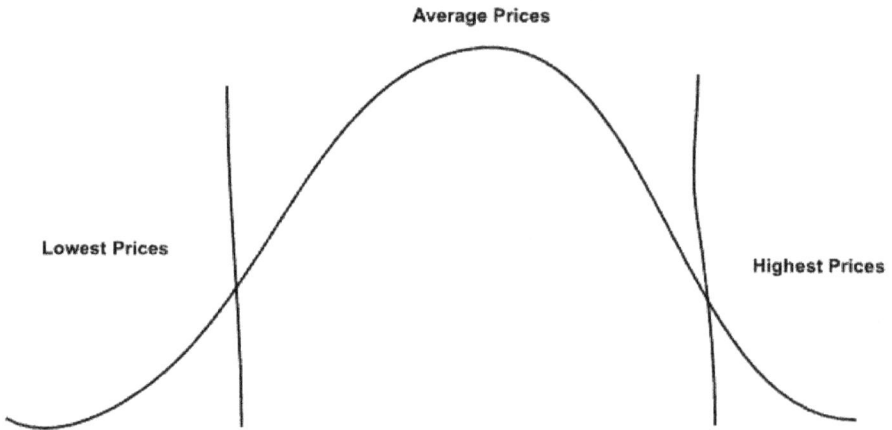

Some of your competitors are going to be on the far left side, the super cheap side. The so-cheap-I-am-not-sure-if-it-is-a-scam side. Sometimes, especially at the start of business, we end up on the far left side as well, the undervalued self side.

This is where people who love deals shop.

The top of the bell curve is where most of your industry pricing sits. This is the average cost of your products and services. This is where most of your competition is priced. The middle section is where most of the population shops. This is where people are generally comparing value, features, result, benefits, and brands.

Then you have the far right side. These are the expensive prices. Most businesses are not pricing this high. This is where you have your high end brands. This side of the price spectrum is where people who care about status and quality shop.

Some people will tell you to avoid the far left side. Perhaps others will say that being on the far right makes a bad person. Still others might say that you need to avoid the center at all costs. There are also coaches and business owners solidly in the far right side camp.

Where do you sit in all of this?

The answer to this question is: it's really up to you.

Where I sit on the pricing bell curve changes depending on what I am selling and what business I am working on. If my brand is a very high-end and exclusive brand, I want to be on the far right of this bell curve. It wouldn't make sense to have a high-end and exclusive brand then sit on the left hand side. That would put up red flags for my fans and I would miss my target market.

If my target market is families with tight budgets, I want to lean slightly towards the left side of the bell curve. If I am trying to attract people with tight budgets, I need to be able to give them prices they can afford.

> Know where you sit in the pricing bell curve and make sure you are sitting there intentionally.

You can also conduct your own pricing research amongst your target market and get a more comprehensive idea of what your market expects to pay for your services.

YOU CAN OUT PRICE YOUR MARKET

When I was a wedding photographer the industry LOVED to tell photographers to raise their prices. Not making enough money? Raise your prices! Have crappy clients? Raise your prices! Working too hard? Raise! Those! Prices!

In their defense most photographers are underpricing themselves. And there is a weird phenomenon where your troublesome clients seem to melt away as you raise your prices. However, raising your prices is not always the solution.

Just because every photographer charges $1000 for a 15 minute session doesn't mean everyone can magically pay it. Charging $10,000 for wedding photography won't work in every area. Charging $5,000 for a single print is not going to work in the foothills of South Dakota.

It is 100% possible to outprice your market. You may find, as you raise prices, you have to reach further and further from where you live to find people who can afford what you offer.

I was traveling between California and Telluride, Colorado to find clients who could afford my services. I had far out priced my immediate market. If you choose to raise prices you need to be aware of what that looks like for your target market.

I work with new business owners. I WANT my services to be affordable for everyone. If I charge $10,000 I am going to miss most of the people I want to help. Most new business owners cannot invest $10,000 into a new business.

Hard stop right here.

You will find coaches out there who claim, "If people want it, they can afford it." They will tell you about the vacations people took, the bags they bought, etc. etc. Apparently, some humans being able to afford vacations means that everyone can afford any price you set. "They will find the money," these coaches say.

Let's get real. That is a fantasy.

Do not be afraid to raise your prices. You *should* be charging what you are worth, you *should* be paid well. You also need to be aware of how price increases are going to impact your target market and therefore your bottom line.

FINANCE THAT FINALLY MAKES SENSE

Create your pricing strategy intentionally. Know that your pricing can support your business, even if you have a slow month. Know that your pricing reflects your brand. And know that your pricing strategy attracts your fans.

Okay, you know your costs. You are accounting for paying yourself. You know how much you have to sell each month to pay all your costs. You know what your profit margin is. AND you know how you compare across the market.

That is so much!

Well, that is only a lot if you did the actual work. If you just read the words but didn't do the work then you don't know those things for your specific business. If we are lucky you have some extra knowledge in your brain. Good job!

Numbers can be confusing, especially as I am just trying to explain this all to you without being in the same room. So, if you are trying to figure out your pricing and need a visual guide, head to my website and download the Money Management Kit. There is a QR code at the end of this chapter.

It is free and each sheet has a little video showing you how to manipulate the numbers in your business for maximum profits.

YOUR CASH FLOW CYCLE

In short, your cash flow cycle is how long it takes for your business to get paid after it puts money out and how long you have cash before you have to spend money again.

Let's say you have a greenhouse. Every year you spend money out to fill your greenhouse with all of the plants. For this example, you are paying out $5000 to fill your inventory.

The amount of time it takes you to recoup $5000 and start making money is your cash flow cycle. You want as much money in your business as you can get. You want the money to stay as long as you can keep it.

177

If you have to wait too long to start making money, you have to float your business and it leads to poor financial situations.

ROUGH CASH FLOW CYCLE

If you have a rough cash flow cycle, you are not getting paid before your business has to put up more cash. In your greenhouse we will say you have to put up your $5000 in February. But, your greenhouse doesn't actually open until April.

This means you have to carry that expense and any others you incur until April. This lack of cash coming into your business makes it hard to pay the bills. It makes it hard to hire employees. When you know you won't see any money until April, it makes it hard to spend money on marketing.

And if you need to feed your family in the meantime, what do you do?

I worked with a hardware store years ago. This hardware store really liked to get the big Christmas deals. Apparently, January is when all of the Christmas vendors/suppliers steeply discount their inventory. My client loved to save the money and would pour his profit from the previous year into these sales.

We all like saving money. And if we are managing our business with personal finance guidelines, this would be a good idea.

As it is, business finance and personal finance are not the same. If this was a personal purchase, he would have saved a large chunk of money and happily moved on. This, however, was a business purchase that he needed to make a profit on.

Steve was purchasing his Christmas inventory in January. When you purchase Christmas in January, you can't start selling it until November. The result was having to float his business for TEN MONTHS before he could start to see a return on his massive investment.

FINANCE THAT FINALLY MAKES SENSE

For years, he ran his business this way, buying discounted inventory and storing it for nearly a year. Every year he was stressed. There never seemed to be enough money for rent. There definitely wasn't enough money to pay himself well. There was barely enough to pay his employees.

This is a rough cash flow cycle. The money is going out, but it is taking ages to come back in and in the meantime, you still have bills to pay.

A HEALTHY CASH FLOW CYCLE

Let's look at this same situation but with business finance guidelines. If we are running our business finance with business in mind, we need to pay attention to cash flow. Again, the mission with your cash flow is to

make money as fast as you can and keep it as long as you can.

With this standard, it doesn't make sense to buy inventory a year in advance then sit on it. You need to make the money back quickly. This business owner could not afford to tie all his profit up in inventory.

The solution was simple. Let go of the discounts.

Steve admitted he rarely, if ever, sold out all of his inventory. He often had to steeply discount his products and sometimes still took losses on them. Not only was he waiting almost a year to make money, but he wasn't making consistent money either.

Steve decided the way to fix his constant cash crisis was to optimize his cash flow cycle. He quit shopping the after holidays vendor sales. He only bought inventory as he needed it and it was ready to go on the shelves. He bought smaller amounts of inventory to reduce the losses he was taking.

Now Steve doesn't have to wait a year to get paid on his investments. He

179

doesn't have to float his business for almost a year. Instead, Steve is cash positive within 20 days of his initial investment. When payroll comes, he pays his people. When rent is due, he has the money to pay it.

SOLUTIONS FOR A ROUGH CASH FLOW CYCLE

If you constantly find yourself in a cash crisis, you might have a cash flow cycle problem. If you know your product/services are priced to make you money but you never seem to have money, you probably have a cash flow cycle problem.

You can do several things if you are needing to fix a cash flow issue. Here are a few options: ask vendors to extend your payment terms, require clients to pay upfront, ask clients to pay a deposit ahead of time, increase your production rate, etc.

If you are having money issues in your business, look at your cash flow. If you are just building your business, you should also be paying attention to your cash flow. How do you optimize when you are getting paid? How do you ensure you always have money coming in? What are your plans to get through the lean months?

Trust me, you do not want to run a business that is always running a month behind and can never seem to catch up.

🪐 FINANCE FINAL WORDS

Before we wrap up finance, I want to do some housekeeping. Here are three things it took me far too long to understand about business finance. I see these mistakes among other business owners daily. Learn from our mistakes.

Hopefully, you catch on a lot faster than I did.

SEPARATE YOUR MONEY

I don't know who needs to hear this *but* you have to separate your money. Your personal money and your business money should not be mixed in the same accounts.You should not be using your personal cards to pay for business expenses. You should not be using your business accounts to pay for personal purchases.

If you bring the wrong card to the store, you need to go home and try again. When you make that awkward walk of shame enough, you stop forgetting the correct card.

If your business is an LLC or Corporation, co-mingling your money (mixing personal and business) can get you in legal trouble. Don't do it.

If you are a sole proprietor, it is not an excuse to mix your money. It is too hard to track your income, to know what you are making, to catch up your accounting, to report expenses. Do not mix your money.

If you are already mixing your money, stop this week. Go get a business checking account. There are plenty of free options.

Keep your business and personal money separate.

CHART OF ACCOUNTS

It took me an embarrassingly long time to know what a business chart of accounts is.

That is how it was with the Chart of Accounts.

Your chart of accounts is two things. One, all your money holding accounts: Venmo, checking accounts, savings accounts, loans, debit cards, credit cards, etc. Easy enough. Two, your chart of accounts also includes your expense and income categories.

I just called these expense and income categories. I just called my accounts, my accounts. So when people asked me, "Do you have your chart of accounts setup?" I had no idea what they were talking about.

One of the biggest problems with understanding business finance is that the vocabulary changes depending on who you are talking to.

Not only that, but many people use the vocabulary wrong – even accountants! So, if you do not know what someone is talking about, ask. Just ask. Ask them to explain to you what they mean. You might know exactly what they are talking about but they are using different words.

This was my problem with my chart of accounts. I didn't know the words.

Your chart of accounts is one of the first steps to setting up your business finance so it can give you information about your business. Sit down with your accounting system and add all of your bank accounts, loans, savings accounts then all of your expense and income categories.

Right there you will be miles ahead of other new businesses.

And if you think you have all of this setup correctly, go double check.

ACCOUNTING SYSTEM

Quickbooks sucks (please don't sue me). Notice the lack of a sarcastrophe. I really do dislike using Quickbooks. I am not a stupid person and I usually don't need a lot of education to figure things out. I can run Photoshop like a pro for goodness sakes, the *original* Photoshop. The one no one understood and you had to pay $3000 just to look at it through your tears while it mocked you.

I can do that. I got that.

I understand basic coding. I know how InDesign, and Flash, and Excel work. Minimal issues.

I cannot figure out what Quickbooks wants from me.

If you are Quickbooks illiterate, like I am, try a more simple accounting system, like Wave or Xero. Both give you all the data and charts you need but also allow you to have a human brain instead of a computer one.

You need an accounting system. Find one that works for *you*. And if Quickbooks is the one for you ^well, may God be with you in Hell^.

Just make sure you have a real accounting system in your business.

YOUR BUSINESS BUDGET

I know you don't want to talk about budgets, but you are hurting your business by avoiding this.

Budgets, when run well, give you freedom.

They allow you to stop feeling like you can't spend money and very quickly tell you where you CAN spend money.

Budgets keep you accountable, in control of your finances, and on the right track to your goals.

Nobody wants to finish up their annual numbers only to realize they made more than they thought but all the money's gone – and they have no idea where it went. A budget helps prevent mysteriously disappearing money. It gives every dollar an assignment. You know where the money in your business is going and even better, you know what strings to pull to keep more money in your own pocket.

Don't let your business run away with all of your money. Make sure you spend real time in finance. Learn how all the pieces of finance work. Get your numbers organized and under control.

NEXT STEPS

Make sure you have a business checking account. Then set up your accounting system and chart of accounts. Create your pricing strategy.

For more help and resources managing your business finances, jump into a Launched workshop. We have a really great live workshop on how to set up Wave. Scan this code or head to the website to get any of the bonuses mentioned in this chapter. This will also help keep you updated on our next Launch Your Business Academy.

Scan the code or visit:
launchedacademy.com/book-bonuses

🪐 CHAPTER 10

NO SYSTEMS, NO BUSINESS

"Good systems give you the power of hiring well."

About a year before COVID shutdown restaurants and businesses all over the world, I had a restaurant hire me. They had recently expanded their building, and took on a bunch of debt to do it.

They expanded in the hopes it would allow them to serve more people, therefore increasing their revenue and most importantly their profit. You see, the owner hadn't taken home a paycheck in over eight years, understandably she was done.

Her family could not keep living to support this restaurant, instead of the restaurant existing to support her family.

She worked her butt off to get funding, building permits, and everything she needed to expand her building. She was featured in SBA newsletters and publications for her drive and accomplishment in her big project. She was a success!!

Except, she still wasn't making more money.

She still wasn't bringing home a paycheck. She still struggled to keep her restaurant running. She just had a bigger, fancier building but all of the same problems.

She reached out to me to tell me what was happening behind the scenes. I told her her problem was systems.

✨ WHAT IS A SYSTEM?

A lot of people think systems are SOPs (standard operating procedures), you know the big, huge book of to-dos for your business. ^The book all your employees read everyday like it is super important to them. The book no one ever puts in the bottom of a drawer and never looks at again.^

SOPs are not a system.

A lot of people think systems are automations. Automations are great! They free up multitudes of time and prevent so many mistakes.

Automations are not a system.

> Your business systems are the streamlined, instinctual, and visual step-by-step processes that outline how everything is done in your business.

Your SOPs and automations are a part of your systems but they cannot be all of your systems.

Let's go back to the restaurant.

When they first hired me to start looking at their systems it was taking approximately five minutes to make a milkshake. If you have ever worked in food you know restaurant time is different from normal time. Five minutes in restaurant time is fifteen minutes in real-people time.

That is too long to make a milkshake. If a family of five came in for milkshakes, five minutes a milkshake means it would take nearly a half an hour just for them to get their shakes! And that is if the restaurant wasn't busy.

Nobody wants to wait half an hour for shakes.

According to the restaurant handbook, the staff was making the milkshake in line with the company's standard operating procedure. The staff was doing everything right. So, why was it taking so long?

There was no REAL system.

The process of making milkshakes had never been streamlined. It was not visual. It was not instinctual. Whatever the opposite of instinctual is, that is what their milkshake making process was. It was "UN-stinctual". The process was ineffective. Nobody had ever looked at how they made milkshakes and thought, "How is the best way to do this?" They just said, "Make a milkshake."

I systematized the milkshake making process. I watched her staff. I timed her staff. I noticed when they were getting confused. I paid attention to all of the times they have to redo steps. I examined the bottlenecks in the milkshake making process. Then I corrected the problems and we did it all again.

Then we did several times after that to test each change.

I created the system to eliminate as many problems as we could. We cut the trips across the kitchen by moving milkshake cups. We cut down the amount of times servers had to read and memorize tickets by adding color coded stickers. We dramatically reduced the amount of time needed to find mix-ins by eliminating the less popular mix-ins as well as moving the high demand mix-ins to a more accessible location.

Everything was moved and systematized with human instinct in mind. Most people are right-handed so cups go on the right side. Most people are not going to remember where they put the cookie dough mix-in so it was given a labeled home with the correct scoop inside.

By the time we were finished we had cut the milkshake making time down from five minutes to less than two and a half. Now that family of five comes in for milkshakes and they get those shakes in less than fifteen minutes. Much better.

Creating the most effective way to accomplish a task and making it easy for anyone to follow is a system. A system is not just saying, "this is how we do things." A system is not just creating automations. A system is creating a process that works quickly and effectively and can be repeated again and again and again.

HIRING POWER

Creating good systems is an entrepreneur superpower! Good systems give you abilities your competition often struggles with or takes far too long to figure out.

Good systems give you the power of hiring well.

I don't know if you have been there yet, but most entrepreneurs go through hiring phases. The first phase is where we know we need someone but we don't know what to do with them. So, we hire because we are drowning. Then we drown together with our new employee. The employee doesn't know what they are doing and we don't know how to train them. Everything is just a lot more work.

Good systems allow you to not only recognize where and when you need to hire, but they help you create amazing training systems so you can have new hires up and working independently in days instead of months. This is phase five, the phase of hiring efficiency and profit. Get to this phase as fast as you can.

QUALITY POWER

Good systems give you the power of quality control! At the pizza place I managed in my teens, there were no real systems. Their "systems" were the basic SOPs that most businesses have. If we were forced to read that handbook before we started working no one remembered a sentence of it.

Like all employees that came before us, we very studiously ignored the giant book of SOPs rotting at the bottom of a filing cabinet.

This meant we all made pizzas our own way.

We all had different pizza priorities. We all thought we were correct and there were no systems to tell us differently. I cared a lot about looks and sauce so I spent a lot of time making sure my sauce was evenly spread and each pepperoni was well placed.

The other manager cared more about speed. His pizzas were more haphazardly thrown together but they were out fast.

Other workers cared about cheese, they had lots of cheese on their pizzas. Still others cared about cost, cheese is one of the most expensive items so they used the smallest amount of cheese possible.

No systems, so we all just did whatever we wanted to.

There was no quality control. Systems give you solid quality control because you can visually show your team exactly what a pepperoni pizza should look like – down to the freaking number of pepperonis on each slice.

LOYALTY POWER

There was no consistency in the food served. Each customer got a pizza but what kind of pizza they got was always a gamble. Sometimes they called in to see who was cooking then decided to eat or pass based on our answer.

As a teen, I didn't realize this was a symptom of bad systems. I just hoped that when people called and I was cooking, they chose to eat with us.

> Your customers do not want to take a risk every time they shop with you.

I don't want to get a great massage one day then a terrible massage the next. I want to know what I am buying. We like consistency and predictability. That is what our brains are comfortable with.

If you have good systems, you can create that oozy and cozy feeling of predictability for your fans. They know what they are getting everytime and they feel safe. That safety is what helps make loyal customers!

They can confidently recommend you to friends. They can confidently get gift cards for gifts. They can comfortably and confidently come back over and over again.

If you do not have good systems, fans will always be taking a risk with your business.

INCOME POWER

Yay money!!

If you have money issues you should probably say that outloud five times.

Yay money!! Say it. I will wait.

Yay money!!

Creating great systems in your business increases your income power for a few reasons. First, it helps you see the holes in your business. When you know where the holes are, you can plug them.

Second, it helps you get more done in less time. If you can get through more customers in less time, you are poised to make more money! If your staff gets more done in less time you are also set to make more money. You are either paying them less or they can take on more customers.

Remember the milkshake restaurant?

> The process of creating and implementing good systems took that restaurant from a $600K business to over a ONE MILLION DOLLAR BUSINESS in less than two years.

PIVOT POWER

The milkshake restaurant hit the one million dollar mark while battling through COVID. They increased their sales through COVID. While other restaurants were shutting down, some for good, this milkshake shop was actively hiring.

What did this restaurant have that made them so different? Good systems.

The leadership team's knowledge of systems allowed them to pivot quickly as COVID-19 took over the globe. Instead of falling back, they stepped up. They had already upgraded their ordering systems, they had simplified their processes, they were running a machine.

Gone were the days when they were constantly at capacity, telling customers they had to wait over an hour for food. They are quick, efficient, and confident. This allowed them to pivot the business.

They shutdown the dining room the business owner originally thought would bring them more income. They changed how people ordered from the drive-in window. They pushed online ordering. They added delivery. They changed the entire business in less than a month. While their competition was hanging "out of business" signs they were hanging "help wanted" signs.

Good systems allow you to pivot when there are problems. If you don't have systems and you also have to pivot, that is a long deep investment dive. You aren't making minor adjustments, you are just pouring fuel on top of a raging fire of chaos.

LESS STRESS POWER

Possibly the most important superpower you get from creating good systems is the power of less stress, of freedom. We all know business ownership can be really hard. Running a business without systems is like swimming in the ocean with shoes on.

> Sure you aren't dead yet but your boots are full of water and they keep pulling you under.

Systems are like floatation devices. They keep you from drowning even when the water gets choppy.

When you have good systems in place, you can let go. You can kick off those water-logged boots and enjoy the beautiful ocean. You can stop fighting your business and enjoy the benefits of entrepreneurship.

The owner of our milkshake restaurant doesn't just take a paycheck now, she has moved away. She doesn't have to work in her restaurant everyday anymore. She doesn't have to fight to stay afloat. She takes home a paycheck doing less work than ever before.

Systems allow you to hand the work off to your team. They allow you to hire well. Systems allow you to expand your business, but most of all systems are what allow you to finally have a life again.

🪐 GOOD SYSTEMS VS BAD SYSTEMS

I have talked a lot about good systems. Let's talk about what makes a system great and what makes it a stinky pile of poo.

Every time I teach about systems I have one smart alec in my class who says, "But even doing it wrong is still a system. No system is still a system." ^Thanks for your deep insights.^ I assume I have smart alec readers as well, so let's talk about it.

Technically, you can say no system is still a system. You can say your chaos is a system.

When I was in high school, I skipped a lot of school. A lot of school.

Sometimes I just hid in my truck in the parking lot (my teachers never looked hard). Other times I recruited friends to join me. On one of the friend recruitment days we went to my friend, Angie's house.

Angie's mother worked so we had the whole place to ourselves. Being fifteen, alone, and bored we decided to make the dessert of all desserts. We started with a brownie mix then added everything sweet or chocolatey we could think of.

There were M&Ms, chocolate syrup, caramel syrup, peanut butter, chocolate chips, and exactly zero discretion.

It was disgusting.

We threw the entire thing in the trash then still had to clean the kitchen so her mom didn't know we missed school. Some smart alec somewhere could say that was a "recipe" but 99.9% of human beings know that is really a slip-into-a-diabetic-coma disaster.

That is how our systems often look, like a complete disaster. Nobody wants to repeat them. Nobody wants to teach them to others. Everything is kind of just a chocolate dessert disaster. Oftentimes, the best thing to do with our system chaos is throw it in the trash.

Call your chaos a system if you want, but much like our dessert of all desserts, we all know what it really is.

ARE YOUR SYSTEMS EFFECTIVE?

Let's dig into what a good system looks like. What are you examining when you look at your systems (or lack thereof)? How do you know if it's working?

The first measurement of a good system is effectiveness. Is your system effective?

If you are packaging products in 60 seconds, everything is wrapped well, labeled well, and ready to go out the door in less than 60 seconds, you might already have a great system. Maybe it doesn't need changing.

But, if packaging products is the bottleneck in your business, we might want to look at what is going on. Why does everything get stopped here? Why does it always feel out of control? Maybe you need more team members. Maybe you are making packaging too hard.

Pay attention to the packaging processes. How many times do you have to walk back and forth? Do you have to search for all the supplies to start packaging? Are you running out of supplies? Do you have to go buy supplies every time you have to pack packages? Do you have to search for the labels?

Now, how do you eliminate overlap?

How do you create a packaging station to simplify and streamline the packaging process? How do you make a packaging station visual and instinctual?

Run through all of the options. Find the holes and the issues in the packaging table. Are your boxes and envelopes on the correct side of the table or do you have to do a lot crossing over and shuffling around to get to them?

Is your packing filler in a place where you can access it without having to put your boxes on the ground or move them out of the way? Are your labels being printed across the room, causing you to walk back and forth constantly? Do you have to pick up the order form multiple times or is it hanging at eye level so you stop losing it?

This is how we start creating a system. We look at a task in our business and figure out why it isn't as effective as we need it to be. Then we add all the pieces to make a beautiful, simple, instinctual system.

SYSTEMATIZE THE LITTLE THINGS

I was a really bad boss for a long time. Okay, not really, really bad but pretty solidly in the "kind of a jerk, yells sometimes, but also fun sometimes, I feel confused about this person so work causes me anxiety" camp. I am not being hard on myself, ask my former team, especially when I managed the pizza place. They will tell you.

> I wanted to be a good boss,
> but I didn't really know how.

I would give everyone a lot of freedom. Then they would do things wrong. I would get upset, I would try to let it go, they would do something else wrong, and my irritation would leak out in little verbal lashes. Then I would feel bad, try to give everyone tons of freedom, and so the cycle would continue.

A huge part of my leadership problem was a lack of systems.

I had SOME things set up but I had focused on the big things.

For years, I was a wedding and portrait photographer. I specialized in prints. Families who came to me ordered prints. I had this beautiful "print pick-up" table in my office. When the big boxes of prints came, we would lay them out on the table, take inventory, take a photo for social media, then package everything beautifully.

No one in my office seemed to get this right.

In five years, I had never had a missing print. Once I handed this off to my staff, we had missing photos all the time.

The prints weren't set up on the table for good photos. Everything looked like chaos. The prints weren't packaged beautifully. The bows were sloppy, the packing slips were missing or a mess, I had no idea which set of prints went to what family.

It was chaos.

And I was *irritated* about it.

How could people be so stupid that they were losing prints? Who doesn't know how to tie a bow? How hard is it to label things correctly? Print day was one of the highlights of my week! *This was supposed to be fun but my team was always messing it up.*

Those are the things I said to myself all of the time. They were not doing it right. They were not smart enough. THEY didn't care.

Here is the truth: I was a bad leader.

I didn't give them the tools they needed to excel at this task. I had five years of figuring it out under my belt. They had five days. And I never taught them how.

I never taught them how because it seemed too small to make a big deal out of.

THE CURSE OF KNOWLEDGE

There is a phenomenon called the curse of knowledge. This phenomenon is what happens when we have known something for so long, we just assume everyone else should know it too. We forget what it was like to not know the things we know.

My sister is a Registered Dietitian. There are a lot of great things in her brain that most of us do not know. She is so smart. She has the degrees and publications to prove it. She knows all about food. She knows it well, and has known it for so long that she is frequently surprised at the lack of knowledge from the rest of us. We don't know things she knows.

However, she went to six years of school to learn what she knows. Of course the rest of the population doesn't know the things she knows. We haven't been studying it for years. She often doesn't remember not having her knowledge so she frequently expects others to have the same knowledge.

This is exactly what I was doing with my poor staff. I assumed everyone knew how to unbox prints. You obviously have to open them from the back so you don't cut the print. The little prints are clearly taped to the inside of the box in an envelope so they don't get lost. Prints obviously have to be arranged at 90 and 45 degree angles or they look like chaos. When you tie a bow you have to go under, not over or it looks droopy.

OF COURSE!

^ What an a**hole. ^

Of course my team didn't know these things. Why would they? This isn't common knowledge. It was knowledge I had to teach myself. I forgot what it was like to not know these things.

I forgot how many times I have to tie and untie bows to get them to look right. I never gave my team a chance.

A good system would have been a step-by-step video of how to open and unbox prints. A good system would be a diagram in the drawer, with the box cutters, to remind them how things are packaged.

A good system would have been a setup guide for displaying and photographing the prints. It would have been a piece of tape on the floor that told them where to stand to get the best photo. It would have been micro grid lines on the table to help them set everything up correctly.

A good system would have been a how to video on tying a bow, with a visual breakdown attached to the ribbon box.

> A good system would have been giving my staff a chance to be great at their jobs. Systems aren't just SOPs in a book somewhere. Systems are available, accessible tools that give our teams their best chance to succeed.

SYSTEMIZING CLIENTS

Did you know you can systematize your clients? Buckle up, this will change your life.

We get so upset when our clients are doing things wrong -- ^oh the audacity of some of these people.^ But, why would they know that isn't how things work in your business? How do they know it takes you three weeks to get orders out?

Oh! You have it somewhere on your website right? In little writing? On one single page? ^Definitely everyone who comes in contact with you has read that. And we most definitely remember it cause it was little and only in one place.^

Be better.

A couple of years ago, I was taking my son to preschool. We arrived to find an array of children standing on the lawn just looking at the front door. It was strange. Just a bunch of three-year-olds staring at their teacher's front door, but not going inside.

I asked my son what he thought they were looking at, he simply said, "The sign is red."

"I am sorry. What are you talking about? What sign?"

"The sign in the window is red. We can't go inside yet."

"When can you go inside?"

"When the sign is green."

This brilliant preschool teacher had systematized toddlers. She gave these kids a simple, repeatable, visual, and instinctive way to know when it was time for class to start. She held strong to her system as well so the kids followed along.

I implemented the same system with my home office within the week.

> If this preschool teacher can systematize toddlers,
> you can systematize your clients.

When you systematize your clients you want to tap into everything my son's teacher did. Make it easy, repeatable, visual, and instinctive. If you create hard systems for your clients, they are going to have a hard time following along.

Make it easy, give them the tools, so they want to follow along. Systematize your client onboarding, your payment processes, your ordering process, etc. etc. This means you are creating systems for every, single one of those processes. You are outlining every single step.

Systemizing your clients means you are kind and clearly walking them through every step of working with you.

VISUAL

I have to admit, it is really hard to teach systems in book form. There is so much more to a good system than just writing down how you do something.

> Creating a visual, instinctive, but also simple process
> is almost an art form.

It's much easier to explain when I show you. That is because humans, in general, are visual learners. 65% of the population are visual learners (Jawed et al. #).

I am one of them.

As a business owner, you are responsible for teaching your future staff. You are also responsible for teaching your clients. If you are not creating visual systems 65% of the team members you try to teach will struggle to understand. This is why a book of standard operating procedures will never be a highly effective training system.

Adding the visual element to your systems doesn't have to be complicated. If you make pizzas, add a diagram of how to make a pizza above the prep table. Add a photo to your cleaning staff's cleaning carts with the layout of how each room should be set up. Put a staff sign behind your welcome sign reminding your team to smile. Add color coded stickers to tickets so they can be understood at a glance.

Do not over complicate any of these steps.

INSTINCTUAL

When we talk about instinctual, these are things like putting the cups on the right side of prep tables, having the right size scoop in pizza sauce, putting labels on everything. If people don't put things away correctly, it is usually because they don't remember where it goes. Add labels. Labels are visual and instinctual. Color coordinate things. Make your team's brains twitch if they do it wrong.

I used to run a short term vacation rental business.

I had a hard time with the cleaning staff putting things away in the right places. Every time we went to check our rental, things were missing. We didn't know if stuff had been stolen, broken, or just misplaced.

I took an entire day to label everything. If you moved the coffee pot, there was a sticker underneath labeled, "coffee pot". Same with the toaster, the blender, and literally everything in that house.

Some might say that is excessive. Maybe it was. However, it triggered a reflex in staff *and* guests. Everyone put things away in the right places. I didn't even train them on it. I never said a word, they instinctively started covering up the stickers with the correct items.

We went from never knowing if anything was missing or broken to being informed in minutes because nobody could handle not covering the stickers. Again, I never trained them on this. It was an instinct.

SIMPLE

Your systems have to be simple to be effective.

Nobody wants to take 25 extra steps each day just for kicks and giggles. Think of the toddlers on the grass. Their "school starts" system was as simple as it gets.

Eliminate the extra steps. Streamline everything. Reduce the times staff need to go find things, double check messages, or walk across your business etc. etc. Good systems are simple.

REPEATABLE

When setting up your systems, you need to make sure it is something that can be repeated. There is no reason to waste your time teaching your crew a very detailed system on how to do something only for them to never need it again.

> There is no reason to setup systems in your business just to abandon them a week later.

Make sure everything you are creating has longevity. You, your team, not to mention your clients need to be able to do these things over and over again.

BUILDING YOUR FIRST SYSTEM WITH P.L.A.N.E.T

We have talked a lot about why you need systems and what a good system is. Creating a great system is a system all of its own.

As small business owners, we often have the urge to jump in and just start creating without a plan. Systemizing your business requires detailed organization and a lot of time. If you jump in without a plan you will likely be swallowed whole.

Think of creating your systems like organizing your house. If you try to organize your entire home at once, you are going to get lost in a pile of clothes, expired pantry items, and kids' toys. There you will be no recovery. You will drown there.

Instead of randomly creating all the systems at once, start smaller. We will use the P.L.A.N.E.T system to help you get your first systems started. In chapter seven we talked about creating a business like a planet for your fans. Here we are going to use the exact same word to help you ensure that your planet is set up to run well.

STEP ONE: PLAN YOUR ROLE

We are going to systematize one role at a time, just like you might organize your home by starting with your pantry. We are going to create a plan. Start your systems journey by defining the roles in your business.

A role is a set of obligations that are related and managed by one person. For instance, a customer service representative is a role in your business. That role would be responsible for the specific tasks and obligations related to customer service.

You probably have more roles in your business than you realize. More than likely, you have been lumping several roles into one big role. ^Your role.^

The problem with this "clumpation" of roles is it confuses responsibility. You end up doing part of your employee/contractor's job; they end up doing parts of your job.

> Tasks get dropped because no one knows
> who is really responsible for them. Chaos and
> frustration ensue.

Your first job, when creating systems for your business, is to write out ALL of the roles in your business, even if you are not looking to hire that role right now. Systems need very clear boxes and organization in order to flourish and add value to your business.

This is the "P" in the P.L.A.N.E.T. system. Before you dive into your systems, you need a plan.

You need to know the roles in your business. Without knowing the roles, it is confusing to get started. You end up creating bits and pieces of systems. And instead of creating a fully functional and amazing machine, you have the beginnings of several machine parts with no way to tie them together.

So, define your roles. And then choose the one you want to start creating systems for.

Some people randomly choose this role while others suggest you systematize the role you dislike the most first. Here is my suggestion: start with your bottleneck.

Where does production in your business get stuck? Where does the money in your business get stuck? What role do you need to improve or add in order to increase revenue?

The places that are keeping your business from growing are what I would systematize first. This allows you to speed up your bottlenecks and begin to outsource the work that is holding you back. Creating systems and hiring correctly is how you expand your business.

STEP TWO: LEARN THE ROLE

After you know your "P", *your plan*, and have chosen the role to systematize, you move to the "L," *learn*. You need to look at the role you chose and learn everything about it. .

This includes defining each task and the obligation for said role. Brain dump every single task this role might be responsible for. Don't filter. Get all the tasks out on paper.

After you have all the tasks written out, we are going to dig a bit deeper. Think about how you would teach these tasks. Determine your foundational tasks; tasks you have to understand before you can learn other tasks.

For instance, you cannot invoice clients until you understand how the accounting system works. You cannot screen print a t-shirt until you have the screen ready for printing, the paint picked out, and the screen set.

Re-order your tasks in order of how they need to be taught. As you do this, also eliminate any tasks that do not fit well into that role.

Then we get to the fun part.

STEP THREE: ANALYZE STEPS

The "A" in P.L.A.N.E.T. stands for *analyze*. You are going to start with one task at a time, the first foundational task. Write out each step required to accomplish said task.

If you need someone to make a bed, you need to write out all the steps to make a lovely bed.

Everyone does not make beds the same way.

Some people have never made a bed. You think everyone knows how to make a bed, but that is shockingly untrue. In addition to not knowing how to make a bed, everyone who can make a bed is *not* going to make a bed *your* way. Just like everyone doesn't tie a bow *my* way. ^Rude.^

You are going to teach them.

Each task needs a list of steps. We are going to assume everyone does not have the same knowledge we have. We are going to assume everyone's mother did not teach them "our way" to make a bed.

Instead of being frustrated or annoyed when your team doesn't do things "your way" we are going to give them the tools they need to succeed.

Here are a few stipulations:
1. If the task has more than ten steps, it is two tasks. You need to break that down.
2. All of your instructions should be simple enough for a ten-year-old to understand.
3. Each step needs to be specific.

If you are teaching someone how to sweep a floor, your steps will not say:

1. Get a broom.
2. Sweep the floor.
3. Put the dirt in the trash.

You are going to say something like:

1. Get the red handled broom from the second cupboard to the right of the sink.
2. Use the broom to "edge" the room: sweep all the dirt and debris from all of the corners and edges of the room.
3. Continue to move all the dirt and debris from the edges of the room into the center of the room.
4. Sweep everything into a small pile.
5. Use the dustpan to collect the dirt and debris. Deposit dirt and debris in the trash can behind the county.
6. Return the broom and dustpan to their correct locations.

Your goal is to be clear, without being condescending.

This is also where you work to streamline your task. Where are steps being repeated? What needs to be added for efficiency? What needs to be removed entirely?

STEP FOUR: NEW TRAINING

The 'N' in P.L.A.N.E.T. stands for *new training*. After you have all the steps lined out for a task, you are going to create new training for it. New training should include but not be limited to:

- Training videos
- Written instructions in places tasks are done
- Visual cues
- Visual reminders
- Instinctual steps

Systems are a process, especially good systems. This is not going to be a quick process. Good systems are going to take time, creativity, and dedication. Just like organizing a pantry, it is going to get messy before it gets better. However, a well systematized business will completely change your growth trajectory. It's worth the time.

This is the place where most business owners stop.

They write out the basic (and boring) standard operating procedures, they put it in a book, no one opens it, then they complain about their employees. Or, they start writing out all the roles and tasks, realize it will take a lot of time to set up and abandon ship. These business owners choose to stay where they are, rather than re-investing in growth.

You can do better. You can go the next mile.

It's going to take time, yet it will be worth it
every minute.

I worked for a department store when I was in college. The training process was a two week event. We watched videos, we shadowed other workers, we were given tests, we were bored out of our minds. The process seemed to go on and on forever. Some trainees quit.

I remember being frustrated with all the training, thinking it was so stupid. I just wanted to get started!!

Then they put me at a register on my own for the first time. Something very strange happened, something that had never happened in all the jobs I had had before. I knew *exactly* what I was supposed to be doing.

I had never experienced confidence like that in a job before. I was always scrambling to figure things out, making stuff up as I went. I made more mistakes than I cared to admit. The first two to three months of a new job were always chaos and stress.

This department store was different. This department store had *systems*. They had a very thorough training system.

It was so well thought out they actually hired more staff than they needed. They knew the percent of hires that would not make it through the training program. They hired six of us. Three of us made it to the end. They didn't have to panic and start over. They didn't have to use more resources to re-train. They knew that 50% of us would quit before the end and they planned accordingly.

Efficiently like that is your goal. You want to have systems that give your people the knowledge they need to be a great asset to your company. My mother and I were recently on a business trip together, we stopped at a cute little burger place along our way.

The girl at the front was very sweet and kind. But when we asked her, "What's good here?" She said, "I am not sure, I am new. I have only had a wrap." When I asked her to recommend a shake, she had the same response. We asked what was on certain burgers, she had to ask. She was trying so, so hard, but the girl hadn't been given the tools she needed.

She had been thrown on the register without training or systems. The business owners just wanted her to figure it out as she went. This was an incredible disservice to not only customers but this girl.

She was not set up to succeed. She was set up to struggle.

> Your employees should be your number one fans.

In order to create number one fans out of your employees you need to give them the tools to succeed. You need to let them taste the food, get real training, and have everything they need to feel confident and sure.

This is never accomplished with a giant company SOP handbook.

You need to be creating P.L.A.N.E.T. training for every system.

STEP FIVE: EXECUTE SYSTEM

The "E" in P.L.A.N.E.T stands for execute. You have created the system, now it's time to put it into action. Putting a system into action does not mean you just created it and walked away.

Putting a system into action means you actually use it.

In order for your systems to keep your business running, you have to be fiercely dedicated to them. This often includes holding more staff meetings to address issues. Your clients are going to try to skip the steps you gave them. Your team will probably do the same. Your role is to hold the line.

Imagine what would happen at the preschool I mentioned earlier if the teacher let even one child in early. If she let one child in while the sign was still red everything would fall apart. She would go from this cute, orderly system to chaos, in seconds.

Your business systems are the same. If you let some bypass the systems, your systems work is worthless. Do not let people skip the training. Do not let your team opt out of the systems. This includes you! Too many business owners think they are the ones who are exempt from the systems.

You are not exempt. Ever.

In order for this to work, you have to hold the line.

STEP SIX: TEST & ADJUST

Your systems will never be "done". Just when you think you have everything figured out, someone's stupidity or creativity *(or both)* will show you a glaring hole that needs a system adjustment.

This is why the "T" in P.L.A.N.E.T. is test.

Technology will change. You will discover a better way to do things. You will release a new product or service. You will have to make changes to your systems and the training that goes with it.

This is to be expected. If you are not regularly testing and adjusting your systems, they will eventually become irrelevant. You will also find that you might not be as clear in your systems as you thought you were. This would also require an adjustment.

Systems need to be evaluated at two times: when they are first implemented and at least annually after that. You will find the most flaws in your systems right at the beginning. You think you created an ultra clear and beautiful system. When others start trying to execute it, you will find the mistakes.

Pay attention, ask questions, learn how to make it better, then make adjustments.

Once you are happy with the system and the training that goes with it, you will want to evaluate those systems regularly. Sometimes evaluations can be as easy as checking with your team. Do they know everything they need to know? Are you getting a lot of the same questions? What mistakes are happening? Where are the holes?

Sometimes it requires running through the whole system again and making adjustments.

TRUST THE PROCESS

This chapter is a lot. I understand that. It can feel overwhelming to get to this point in your business. Systems are a lot of work that require a lot of organization. They also take commitment. Do not stop here.

There are multiple reasons only 15% of business owners make it to $100,000. Not being able to implement the correct systems is one of those reasons. You have to let go and trust the process.

The sooner you can implement systems in your business, the faster and easier your business can grow. Most business owners do not make it to this point and to be candid, I hate coaching on systems because very few business owners are willing to do what it takes.

Most business owners I have coached in systems are not prepared to look at what they are doing wrong. They are not willing to admit that they are the problem. They feel like they are babying their team, making things too easy, adding more work on their already too full plate. The argue through every step of the process.

Honestly, I get it.

I have been frustrated with employees before too. I have felt the strain and irritation of having to stop what I am doing to walk a team member step-by-step through something as simple as packaging a box..

I have lashed out at team members for not being able to figure it out on their own. How do they think I learned it? I freaking figured it out!

However, employees and contractors are not business owners. They didn't sign up to "figure it all out." *You* did. When you started your business, you signed up to be the person with the answers.

> If you want your business to grow, you have to
> start creating the systems so that other people can
> help you.

Systems are a hard stop for many business owners, even owners who are drowning. They have been doing things "their way" for years. Creating systems means letting go. They have to let go of micro-managing. They have to let go of doing everything themselves. Business owners frequently have to let go of some pretty powerful victim mentality.

Setting up systems that work means you have to admit the problems in your business are your fault. Clients not paying you on time, that's a you issue. Employees not doing a great job, also a leadership issue. Creating systems requires making a mess of your business while you re-organize. It also means standing up and taking responsibility for everything that happens in your business.

If you are in a position where you feel like you are stuck in your business where you can't seem to get out of the frantic or famine cycle, systems are probably your solution. You can do that hard work and fix the problem. It will probably take you a good year. Or you can keep going the way you have been going. The choice is up to you.

If your business is still relatively new, CONGRATULATIONS!! This is the best time to start setting up systems in your business. If you can set up systems now, at the beginning, you can avoid the giant mess and all of the mistakes and costs that come with having to set up a system 5, 10, or 20 years into the future of your business.

This is why I push system creation so hard in my new business owners. If you wait, most of you will not make it. I want you to make it. I *really* want you to make it.

Create great systems for your business to grow on. Give your team the tools they need to succeed. Give your business the foundation it needs. A chaotic business has a growth limit. None of us want a growth limit.

🪐 HOW TO MAKE HIRING AN ASSET

Now that you generally understand systems, I think it's only right that we talk about hiring. After all, your team will be the ones who use your systems the most.

When I talk about hiring, I am referring to employees *and* contractors. I understand employees and contractors are not the same, but you still need systems for both. You need to make sure your business standards are being upheld and your brand is being represented correctly.

HIRE OR CAP OUT

Whether you want to hire or not, the facts remain: if you do not hire your business is capped. You will reach a point in your business where you cannot grow on your own anymore. Don't be upset or mad at me, this is the math.

> You only have so many hours in a day. You don't get extra hours.

We all have the same amount of time in a day. There are only twenty-four in a day. That's it. When you have used all the time available to you, your business is capped. The only way for it to grow, is to add team members to your business.

There is no getting around it.

WHAT IF I CAN'T AFFORD TO HIRE?

I am often asked this question. "What if I can't afford to hire?". To which I always reply,

> can you afford *not* to hire?

Stay with me.

A lot of business owners hear "hire" and immediately think that means taking money out of their own pockets and giving it to someone else. In order to hire, they have to take a pay cut. This is only true when you don't understand *how* to hire.

You have two options when you hire help: hire for growth or hire for time.

Hiring for growth means that you make more money because you added a team member. This person allows your business to make more money. They are helping you expand production, they are taking on additional client work, or maybe they are a salesperson bringing in more work.

This is the kind of hiring I like. I want to hire for growth.

Typically, hiring for growth is what other business owners want as well. Nobody wants to take a pay cut in order to add a team member.

HIRING IN THE RIGHT PLACES

The key to hiring for growth is to make sure you are hiring in the right places.

Let's say Harry Heartthrob is swamped in his business. All of his orders are late, every day feels like chaos, and he doesn't think there is an end in sight. Even though Harry is a tough dude, he sometimes cries into his woodworking because his business feels so heavy.

Even though he is backed up on orders, he is barely making enough for his family. He often feels he has to give discounts for late work. He makes mistakes because he is so stressed out. He is also working significantly more hours than he did at his corporate job.

Harry Heartthrob asks for support – I tell him he needs to hire.

Like so many other business owners, Harry doesn't think he can afford help. He is barely making enough for his family, how can he pay someone else?

Let's do the math!!

Not sarcastically, I love math. Math is concrete, math isn't guesswork. Math is awesome.

If Harry hires Buddy Bumble to work in his woodworking shop for 40 hours a week, he will get 40 hours of time back. Let's say he pays his new hire $25/hr while his woodworking shop charges $40/hr. Each week he is paying $1000 for help. Harry, of course, hears these numbers only to repeat the epithet, "I can't afford help." His family cannot live on $600/week.

But wait! There's more!

What is Harry going to do with his 40 hours?

Harry can choose to do whatever he wants with those 40 hours. He can take a nap, he can clean his shop, he can catch up on his books. Harry chooses to split his time. He spends 10 hours working on marketing, 20 hours helping his hire keep up in his shop, and 10 hours with his family.

In the 10 hours that Harry spends on marketing he is able to make three more sales a week. Each sale brings in a revenue of approximately $800.

With his time and his Buddy's time in the shop, Harry Heartthrob's Hardwood can keep up with all the new orders. This means Harry no longer feels obligated to offer discounts for late orders. He is also making fewer mistakes because he doesn't feel like he is drowning.

The lack of discounts coupled with the lack of mistakes is saving him $200/week.

Let's add that all together. Harry's revenue has increased by $2,400/week. He already had the income to pay Buddy, with $1,400 left over. Plus, he saved $200 on mistakes. Suddenly, Harry Heartthrob's revenue increases by $1,600.

That is $83,200 every year. How much money Harry is leaving behind when he chooses to continue to kill himself in his shop alone instead of getting help. $83,2000!

Just by hiring help and using his time well, Harry Hearthrob has added nearly one hundred thousand dollars to his bank account. Even if Harry only gets two sales each week instead of three, he is still coming out on top.

This is hiring for growth. By adding Buddy to his team, Harry was able to

DON'T SUCK AT BUSINESS

immediately grow his business.

Here is the math formula for your business.

[hired time] x [pay rate] = [weekly payroll]

[new time available] / [hours to make one sell] = [sales in a week]

[sales in a week] x [average sell revenue] = [weekly revenue increase]

[weekly revenue increase] x 52 = [annual revenue increase]

Don't understand this math?
Jump in a Launched workshop and we will walk you through it.

WHEN HIRING FEELS LIKE A MISTAKE

When I was running my photography studio poorly, I often found myself feeling a lot like Harry Heartthrob at the beginning of his story. I was working endless hours. I was exhausted. I cried into my photography.

Unlike Harry, I didn't do the math before I hired. I hired blindly. I hired desperately.

"Experts" I believed were much smarter than me told me to hire a team. Hiring was supposed to get me out of the frantic or famine cycle.

So, I hired. I hired and I lost $20,000. I hired someone different and my family took another $20,000 pay cut. Everytime I brought someone into my business my family lost money.

It sucks to write an employee a check for more than you make.

It is gut wrenching to pay your employees knowing
that there will be nothing left for your family once they
all cash their checks.

216

Yet, that was my reality for years.

I just couldn't figure out what I was doing wrong.

I have told this story thousands of times to hundreds of business owners. In all my years of sharing it only one other business owner could tell me why I wasn't making any money.

Afterall, the math above proves that if you hire, you make more money. We are leaving money on the table if we refuse to bring on a team. That is all true – *if* we are hiring in the right places.

When I hired in my photography studio, I was hiring for time. Every time.

I was booked solid. I had clients up to six months out. I couldn't take any more work, even if I wanted to. I was already priced so high, I frequently had to travel 2-6 hours for work (one way). I was capped out.

> There was no way for me to bring anymore money
> into my business.

Each time I hired, I hired someone to help with office work. They responded to emails, sent bills, unpackaged prints, or helped me on a photoshoot. They were not revenue producing. My team was really nice to have (most of them) but they did not bring additional income into my business.

HIRING IN THE RIGHT PLACES

I was hiring in the wrong place.

If I wanted less work and more money, I needed to hire for growth. I needed to hire someone that would allow the business, not me, to take more work. Someone answering emails did not allow me to take more work.

I didn't need an office manager, I needed another photographer. Or, perhaps,

I needed another photographer and an office manager.

Another photographer would have allowed me to double the revenue coming into my business. Another photographer would have allowed my business to grow. Another photographer would have allowed us to take on more clients. We could be at two weddings at once. This would have taken time off me, paid for the second photographer, and put more money in my pocket.

When you start to hire, you need to look at where you are hiring.

> What roles will allow you to grow, and what roles will just allow you to go home an hour early?

And hey, if going home an hour early is what you want from a hire, that is great! Make sure you understand that you will be taking a pay cut for that hour of time you get back.

Sometimes, hiring a business manager or assistant is the way to grow your business. Perhaps you have no time for marketing. Hiring someone to take menial tasks off your to do list so that you have time to create amazing marketing and take sales calls, does allow your business to grow.

MATH DOESN'T LIE

If you run the math formula above for your business and you are not making significantly more money by hiring, you are hiring the wrong position. I have run this system with more business owners that I can count. Nine out of ten of them will double or triple their income by bringing on help.

> Frequently, doing everything themselves was the single thing keeping business owners from million dollar revenue marks.

You are not the only person who can do the things that you do. I am sure that you are great. I am sure your clients love you. However, if you want to grow, really grow, your business, you are going to have to let go of the control and train others to do what you do.

The math doesn't lie.

You will eventually be capped out on your own time. Perhaps you have already hit that point. The only way to get more time is to bring on team members.

Create the systems that you need to grow. Find your growth bottleneck and let go of doing everything yourself.

> If you want massive growth in your business, you are
> going to have to change the way you do things.

NEXT STEPS

Do the math. What would you make in your business if you could fix your bottlenecks? What would you make in your business if you could stop doing little tasks and focus on your area of genius?

Define the first role you should hire.

For more help and resources on setting up your systems and figuring out how to hire, jump into a Launched workshop. Scan this code or head to the website to get any of the bonuses mentioned in this chapter. This will also help keep you updated on our next Launch Your Business Academy.

Scan the code or visit:
launchedacademy.com/book-bonuses

CHAPTER 11
GO FURTHER FASTER

"Collaboration benefits should not be ignored."

Small business owners are not fantastic collaborators. I want to change that. Many small businesses have done collaboration the wrong way one too many times. They are sick of wasting time and money.

I get it. We are not in business just to help everyone else and never make money ourselves.

With that said, *good collaboration* can take your well-run business and absolutely skyrocket it.

Good collaboration increases your assets while expanding your fan base. Good collaboration can change your business for the better.

Collaboration is a mutually beneficial project between two or more businesses or entities. *This is not just doing another business a favor.* That is just doing a friend a favor. Collaboration is a project where both businesses/entities benefit. Yay for everyone making money!

Collaboration is clearly outlined. Collaboration is not one business doing all of the work while the other reaps most of the benefits. Collaboration is not sponsoring an event. That is just marketing. Collaboration is not throwing your logo on the back of a t-shirt. Collaboration improves all businesses involved and the work is shared or compensated accordingly.

WHAT DOES COLLABORATION LOOK LIKE?

I love a good collaboration. I love it even more when it's a good collaboration between small business owners. Knowing what a good collaboration looks like can be hard to identify at first. Let's start by clearing it up.

In a small town in Arizona there is a mortuary. Like most mortuary websites, family and friends can get online, learn details about memorial services and leave condolences for the family. This small mortuary took it one step further.

They partnered with their local flower shop to offer floral arrangements on their website as well. Family and friends from all over the world can visit the site and send flowers to the mourning family.

This idea is not original. This small town mortuary did not invent this collaboration. But here is why I like it. This is a local partnership. The flower shop and the mortuary are both benefiting. They are also both expanding their services, helping increase their public relations, and adding value to their community and clients.

221

This collaboration took a little work, websites had to be connected, an ordering system had to be set up, and arrangement options had to be created. But it is a simple example of teamwork and small businesses supporting small businesses.

COLLABORATION BENEFITS

While many small business owners like to ignore collaboration and focus on marketing instead, there are massive benefits to collaboration. Collaboration benefits should not be ignored. Networking and building professional relationships will absolutely change your business. Great collaborations also make your marketing easier.

Think of it this way. If you spend 10 hours looking for clients and get one new client, you have one new client. If you spend 10 hours looking for collaborators and find one great collaborator, you have someone who will send clients to you again and again and again.

92% of consumers, your potential clients, trust reviews and recommendations from others more than they trust your marketing. Good collaboration is oftentimes much more effective than your own marketing.

And 91% of millennials are willing to try a new brand if they learned about it from someone else. NINETY-ONE percent. (Howarth)

> You are not the best lead generator for your business,
> other people are.

Get out there and find them.

Before you get out there and find these great collaboration partners, you need to know what you are looking for. If you don't know exactly what you are looking for you will meet a bunch of weirdos (like me) and never know how to take the next step with them.

Just like we market with intention, we also collaborate with intention.

Know the type of collaboration you are looking for before you start looking. Know what type of business or person would make a good partner, what your benefits are, and what the benefits are for your collaboration partners.

🪐 TYPES OF COLLABORATION

There are several types of collaborations out there. You don't have to catch them all. Choose the one that works best for you right now.

INFLUENCERS

Influencer collaborations used to be limited to celebrities and athletes most of us would never have access to. Social media created an influencer industry. Now any business owner has options to include influencers and micro-influencers in their marketing plan.

Let's say, Sally is trying to sell her seashells to another seashore. Collectors don't come to the seashore to buy her shells anymore. She knows she needs to start shipping. But Sally doesn't have a huge client base yet. She hasn't been collecting emails or growing her social media for the last 114 years.

Sally can use websites, like Upfluence, to find influencers with followers who love seashells but don't always make it to the seashore. These influencers can teach their audience all about Sally and her amazing seashells.

Instead of trying to reach 1,000 new clients on her own, Sally can reach 30,000 collectors faster, with just a little help. And like we talked about before, people will trust these influencers more than they trust Sally. So, not only can Sally have a greater reach, the efforts are likely to have a better ROI (or return on investment, the money you make from your investment). Yay money!

AFFILIATE

The second type of collaboration is an affiliate partnership. This is similar to influencers but affiliate offers are not exclusive to influencers.

An affiliate is someone companies pay to send their friends, family, and acquaintances to said business. Lots of businesses have affiliate programs. Typically, anyone can join. They get a special link or coupon code. Every time someone uses their link or code, they get paid. Who doesn't want to get paid just for sending your favorite people to your favorite businesses?

I love this option because I can reward my amazing clients just for talking about me to their friends. My biggest fans are already doing that. Now, they just get a bonus for it.

With influencer marketing you have a large amount of control over what the influencer posts about your business. Creating content is typically a team effort. Affiliate marketing, however, is very hands off. You don't control what is being said or shared about your business.

You simply pay for the results.

NETWORK

Network collaborations are all about expanding your circle of people. This is where spending your time at networking groups comes in. Many new business owners go to networking groups to try and sell their products/services. They are doing it wrong.

While you might pick up a client or two at a networking group, you should be focusing on finding incredible referral partners for your business.

When looking for a network collaboration you should be looking for a business that offers a product or service complimentary to yours. Let's say you teach brave humans how to rappel. A very great referral partner for you would be an outdoor adventure company or a river rafting company. A company that sells the gear you use would be amazing as well.

You are looking for businesses where you can refer seamlessly back and forth. It would be weird for a rappelling teacher to tell someone where to buy Christmas decorations. It would be useful for a rappelling teacher to tell someone where to buy rappelling gear.

These network (or referral) collaborations are highly valuable because they send you high value leads. These are not people casually posting to a random audience about what you do, these are other companies knowing what their customer needs next and sending them to you with money in hand.

Do not sleep on building your network.

Some businesses have referral partners or network collaboration kickbacks. Essentially, they pay you to send business their way. Those are always great benefits to add to your networking.

ALLIANCES

Alliance collaborations are some of my favorites. An alliance collaboration is when two (or more) businesses get together to market their products and services as a team. They split the cost of their advertising combining resources, and marketing budgets.

This type of collaboration is often seen from big corporations. Think of anytime a big movie comes out and suddenly it is everywhere!

"Why get a regular drink when you can get a drink with images from this big, important movie all over the cup?"

"See this cool car? It has actors from this big, important movie inside it. Buy both!"

"Big, important movie themed fro-yo! I know you want it, it tastes better with big, important movie flavors."

Big corporations are phenomenal at this type of collaboration. Small businesses should be as well. Flex your collaboration muscles and start looking for ways to combine promos with other business owners. Who compliments your service/product?

Who can add that bit of flare to your next launch?
Get creative!

This type of collaboration works best when you are promoting an upcoming event. A product launch, a sale, a masterclass, etc. Think of the event you want to promote then make a list of the collaborators you could work well with to promote it.

You want collaborators who share your target market, can expand your reach, are not in competition with your products/services, and have resources to share.

This could be as complicated as a full scale marketing campaign or as simple as a podcast interview.

PORTFOLIO

The last type of collaboration is portfolio collaboration. This is when you add a new product or service to your business by outsourcing it to another company.

Let's say you own a custom t-shirt shop. You do custom screen printing for youth teams, small businesses, and schools. If they need swag, you've got it. Then someone asks if you can do embroidery.

Your business doesn't offer embroidery. You don't know how to add that service, you don't have the equipment, and you definitely don't have the space for it. Cue portfolio collaboration.

> Instead of turning down the work or scrambling to learn a new skill, you simply find the right vendor to do the project for you.

Typically, when you create a portfolio partnership, you are looking for a business who will white label their work for your company. When something is white labeled it means it's branded to look like it came directly from your company. Oftentimes, you can also get better rates because you are sending your new collaborator a lot of work.

These collaborations allow you to offer more to your customers without having to add the actual service to your business. Frequently, you offer a service your portfolio partner doesn't offer in their own business so they can send work to you as well.

The collaboration increases revenue on multiple levels and is a very easy way to grow your business.

FINDING THE RIGHT PARTNERS

There are many ways to add collaboration partners to your business. Choose the one that feels best to you then get started. You don't have to grow your business alone, and honestly, you shouldn't.

You want to look for a few specific things when you are searching for your ideal collaborations.

SAME TARGET MARKET

You need to make sure your collaboration partners share the same ideal target market as you. If your fans are women in their 50s who are struggling with

DON'T SUCK AT BUSINESS

being empty nesters, it does not make sense to partner with a business who serves 20 something men who like video games.

Make sure your collaboration partners are working to attract the same type of target market you are working to attract.

This way you can both easily expand your reach! Let's say your collaboration partner has an audience of 3000 and you have an audience of 3000. When you pull both your audiences together

you are reaching twice as many fans
than you were on your own.

COMPLIMENTARY PRODUCTS

You do not want collaboration partners who are your competition. ^I know, I know, "collaboration over competition."^ That does not apply to your marketing for one simple reason, it is confusing to your potential clients.

Disney has often collaborated with McDonald's. That makes sense to most of us, we get cool Disney toys at McDonald's. I love that. Kids love that. Disney toys in a McDonald's happy meal make sense.

How would you feel if McDonald's chose to do a collaboration with Burger King? What if you got a Burger King crown in your happy meal? Or a whopper?

That doesn't make a lot of sense. Everybody would be a little confused. At least one marketing dude would be instantly fired.

It is the same with your business. If you are running collaborations with businesses who are in competition with your business, your potential clients will be confused. We don't take action when we feel confused.

Make sure your collaboration partners have complimentary products not competitive products.

BENEFITS YOUR BUSINESS

Before you jump into any collaboration you are offered, make sure it benefits your business. It's great to do service and help others, but that is not a business collaboration. That's just doing something nice for someone.

If you are working on creating collaborations to build your business, you need to ensure those collaborations are benefiting your business.

Ask yourself how you will turn revenue from this project. How long will it take to turn revenue? How will this collaboration expand your reach? How will you measure your success?

If you don't know the answers to these questions, you need to do some homework before you jump into the collaboration.

🪐 FINDING GOOD COLLABORATIONS

It can feel hard and a little nerve wracking to get started when you are adding collaborations to your business. Here is the general system I follow to make sure I am bringing in collaborations that are not only pushing my business forward but also the business of my collaborators.

STEP ONE: SOLID OFFER

Before I start reaching out to anyone, I want to know what my offer is and how it benefits them. I really hate the collaboration meetings that go,

"Hey! It looks like we could be great collaboration partners! Here's everything

I do. What about you."

"Me too! Here's all the things I do."

"Cool! Wanna collab?"

"Sure! How do you want to do this?"

"I don't really know. I might have an affiliate program. It isn't great though."

"I was thinking about one too. Will you just send my workshop to your email list?"

"Oh, okay..."

This isn't good collaboration. It is a waste of everyone's time. Business owners are busy, none of us have time for these calls. If you are going to ask someone to help you push your business to their audience they need something in return.

> Collaboration is NOT blasting your email list with other people's stuff.

Collaboration is two (or more) entities working together, pushing both businesses. Do you feel like I am repeating this a lot? It is because I am. This is the single most important part of a collaboration.

Before you reach out to a potential collaborator, have a great offer. Great offers include: Will you be on my podcast, can you teach a workshop, do you want to create an ad highlighting both our services, can I white label your services sending you more work, etc. etc.

Have an offer. Know what you get and what your collaborator gets.

STEP TWO: WHAT RESULTS ARE YOU LOOKING FOR?

Know what results you want from the collaboration. Before you reach out to

230

potential collaborators, know what results you want. Do you want to make $10,000? Do you want to create some viral videos? Do you want an increase in sales, if so, how many?

What do you need?

Knowing what you are looking for in the collaboration helps each partner manage expectations. This also helps everyone know your collaboration is a project they feel they can contribute to. If you are looking for 1000 additional Instagram followers yet your collaboration partner is happy if you get 10, you are not on the same page.

Know your expectations. Get on the same page.

STEP THREE: A GREAT OFFER SHOULD BE CLEAR

Make sure you are hyper clear with your collaboration offer. Highlight the time it will take you and your partner, when they will start to see results, how many times you will meet, and what their return might look like.

Take time to ask what results they would like in a collaboration. And always, always set a timeline you are both willing to adhere to.

Be clear about the next steps and what value your collaboration can bring to their business or organization. Every collaboration should have a general contract outlining what is expected from each party.

TRACK. TRACK. TRACK.

Tracking collaborations is just as important as tracking your marketing. Collaborations are marketing after all.

In order to know which collaborations are working for you and which collaborations are just draining your time, energy, and resources, you need to track them. Do not waste your time doing collaborations that don't yield results.

Prepare to track collaborations from the
very beginning.

WHAT DO YOU TRACK?

You want to make sure you are tracking the progress of the collaboration. Who is waiting on whom? What are the next steps? Who needs to sign off on any assets. Know where you are in the collaboration process at any given time.

I love a good spreadsheet or a project management system for this. I used to be able to keep everything in my head. But I am old now and actually aware of my limitations. Use the tools available to you to create tracking that will yield success. You need a tracking system all collaborators can use.

You will also need to track the results of the collaboration. You want to know how much money was made for each party, how far your collaboration reached, the cost of the collaboration, the time commitment, and the leads brought in.

I understand this is a lot. I have created a spreadsheet to help you track all of this. You don't have to know everything or be good with numbers, I have done the hard work for you. ^Feel free to thank me in the form of one million dollars.^

REVIEW RESULTS AND MAKE ADJUSTMENTS

Tracking is useless if you don't look at the data! Make sure you track well. Then review your data and make the appropriate adjustments. You will not get this right the first time. It might take you several tries before you figure out how to make collaborations flourish.

If you are not tracking your collaborations, figuring out how to make them raging successes is going to be a giant guessing game. You don't know what you need so you keep trying everything, spreading yourself too thin, and losing a lot of money.

One bad collaboration doesn't mean every collaboration is a waste of your time. Review your tracking results, make adjustments, and try again.

Don't give up.

You can do hard things.

NEXT STEPS:

Brainstorm the type of collaborations you would like in your business. Who would be a great referral partner? What would a great affiliate program look like?

For more help and resources on creating solid business collaboration, jump into a Launched workshop. Scan this code or head to the website to get any of the bonuses mentioned in this chapter. This will also help keep you updated on our next Launch Your Business Academy.

Scan the code or visit:
launchedacademy.com/book-bonuses

🪐 CHAPTER 12
COURAGE IN BUSINESS

"I now run a business that doesn't only support me financially, it supports me as a human being."

Healing myself and my body from the chronic stress that came with managing my business poorly, was not an easy mission. I have had to learn to look at business in a completely different way.

I had to go from creating a business completely centered around me and my skills, to a business where I was unnecessary. This change forced me to see business from a higher level. At this level I was looking down on my business, analyzing it. I was creating a machine that could produce predictable

234

results over and over again. A machine where I wasn't in the middle, gumming everything up.

Making the shift to a sustainable business was hard. The next five years of my life required intense courage and constant growth. Apparently, I am super arrogant because the idea of not needing to be the central piece of my business was a pill I choked back up several times.

It was worth it. I now run a business that doesn't only support me financially, it supports me as a human being. I have helped other business owners create the same thing. I can take time off. I can have a sick day. Twice in the last nine months I spent weeks abroad. I was able to spend a month in France with my family. I didn't work the whole time I was there either. I did little to no work at all.

My business reliably and consistently provides for my family. I don't work 12-18 hour days. I have a hard time getting a full eight hours in. I spend most of my summer on the lake with my kids and husband. I have time for family events. I am a part of my life again! I am a part of my kids' lives again.

For once, when I ask myself, "Kara, what are you doing with your life?" I have an answer. It's an answer I am very, very proud of.

It has taken me way longer than I would like to admit to get to this point in my life, to get to this point in my business. It was a hard path. It was a long path. Changing the way I ran business was hard. Growing personally was hard. The harder part was continuing to move forward when everything looked hopeless.

My family and I had some really bad days as I went through this learning process. There were so many times I wanted to quit. So many times I thought I should quit.

> Knowing how to bounce back when your business journey looks impossible is vital to your business success.

The path before us often looks hard and daunting. The trick is not to eliminate hard and daunting, the trick is to knowing how to keep moving forward.

DIVING IN

Remember my photography studio? When I started my studio I jumped in head first.

I went to one of the biggest bridal shows in the country, set up a booth, and sold my photography services all day. I booked two years of weddings.

I didn't have much experience. I was brand, freaking new, but I knew what I wanted. I was terrified. I had never photographed a wedding before, yet I was asking couples to let me photograph theirs! ^the nerve of me.^ I wasn't fearless, I was just fiercely determined. I knew what I wanted and I dove in.

I am not an amazing salesperson. I wasn't more talented than the other photographers at the show. I was less talented than many. I was also impatient. I believe business owners don't have time to wait for things to happen TO us. We have to make things happen FOR us.

I don't believe we have time to wait for things to be perfect. The "right time" is a myth. I don't even believe in building giant portfolios or "paying our dues."

> We have bills to pay right now!! We have businesses
> to build.

I quit my job to start my photography business. I didn't ease into my photography studio. I just quit my job deciding I would make it work or starve. I didn't have time to "get my name out there" or to beg for each client. I found the place where I knew my clients were, and I went for it. That place was bridal shows.

I didn't know what I was doing. I was scared, I was full of doubt. I was making

236

it all up as I went along. But I think doing hard things is what courage is in the end. I think courage is being unsure, imperfect, and afraid, then big-fat doing the scary thing anyway.

FEAR IS REAL

I opened my photography studio over 14 years ago. Since then, and several businesses later, I have had to do a lot of scary things. I have had to make sales calls. I have had to call lawyers over legal issues. I have had months with no sales. I have had hard conversations with furious clients. I have had to grow and change myself.

Facing the person in the mirror always takes courage.

I have cried myself to sleep. I have had more nightmares than I can count. I have been so stressed I couldn't sleep at all. I have dry heaved in public restrooms, thrown up in parking lots, and hyperventilated in my car.

I have embarrassed myself a lot. A lot, a lot. So many times have I publicly embarrassed myself.

Here's the important part: all stories start with failure, struggle, and obstacles. Nobody wants to read a story about some schmuck who dropped on Earth, had a perfect life, never made mistakes, and never had anything to overcome. ^He just existed and therefore life was golden. Angels sang, women swooned, his castle was built.^

Ew.

None of us want to read that story because we know it isn't real. Struggles, failures are part of life. We all have struggles. We will all make massive mistakes. We did not drop onto this planet with all the knowledge and skills we needed to be our best selves. We were not born with the knowledge to make millions. We have to cultivate those skills. Cultivating requires some struggle.

It is time we gave ourselves permission to struggle.

> It is time we gave ourselves permission to become the people we are meant to be.

"WANNABU" STATEMENTS

I have worked with hundreds and hundreds of business owners. Almost all of them have big dreams. They know what they want, they see what it can be, and they are so incredibly capable. More often than not, there is only one thing between where they are now and where they want to be.

That one thing is themselves.

Yes, themselves. They are holding themselves back. They are keeping themselves stuck. I know that that sounds harsh but I have seen it repeatedly. I have also been very guilty of standing in my own way.

I hear it almost everyday, "Yes, I want to but…"

"I am afraid to let go."

"What if I fail?"

"What if I have too much work and can't keep up?"

"I'm waiting for the right time."

"I have to do all the research, all of it, first."

I call this a "wannabu" statement; I want to but…

We know what we want, we know what it looks like, but we set our barriers in the way. We keep ourselves stuck. We let our fears and our worries keep us stalled in the same place year after year, after year.

Most people will fight this theory. We don't want a wannabu. We don't want to admit we are keeping ourselves stuck in our current cycle. It's so much easier to blame others or to blame our situation. ^I know in my life I am 100% not to blame for any of the junk that happens to me. I make good choices and love Jesus.^

> We don't want to take the blame. We want to move forward. We want to reach our goals. And yet, we are still stuck.

Here are three questions you can ask to check your wannabu statement. These will tell you really quickly if *you* are the thing keeping yourself stuck. The elements of a wannabu statement are threefold. If you can't answer them all with a solution, you are allowing yourself to be the biggest barrier in your success.

First things first. Identify what you think is holding you back. Why haven't you launched your business yet? Why is your business not growing? If you are feeling stuck or impatient with your progress, what is the cause of your overall stuckness?

Can you not write a book because you don't have time? Is your business struggling to make money because your friends and family are not supportive?

Identify what you feel is keeping you where you are, then ask the following questions.

QUESTION ONE: WHAT ARE YOU DOING ABOUT IT?

Let's say Sally's wannabu statement is that she wants a 100K+ following on social media before the end of the year. Her barrier is that she doesn't know what to post.

So we ask the questions, what is she doing about it?

Is she learning more, creating content, and testing what works? Or is she spending a lot of time watching TikTok videos wishing things were better for her? Is she researching endlessly but not taking action?

If you are not taking action, real action, towards your goal, you *fail* this question. If you are taking real and *consistent* action to fix the problem, you pass. Planning is not action.

QUESTION TWO: WHAT IS YOUR PLAN?

The second question is: what is your plan? Sally doesn't really have a plan. She just watches TikToks hoping to be struck with inspiration. She is waiting for things to change somehow. She is waiting for strangers to suddenly follow her for exactly zero reason.

> She doesn't have a next step. She is perpetually
> just hoping.

She also fails this question.

What about you? What plan do you have to leap through your obstacles? What are you going to do to change your outcome? If you have a plan, a real plan, you pass this question. If you don't have a plan, you also fail.

QUESTION THREE: HOW ARE YOU TAKING CONTROL?

The last one is, how are you taking control? If Sally doesn't have a plan to reach her 100k followers, how is she taking control of the situation?

Has she signed up for a class that will help her write a plan? Is she taking the steps to free up time for more content writing? What are any of us doing to take control of our circumstances? What are we doing to make sure we are moving closer to our goals?

If you ask yourself this question and realize you are doing nothing to take control, you fail this question.

If you failed any of these three questions, the thing standing in your way – is you.

DON'T BLAME ME

Now right about here, I get business owners saying things like, "You don't understand. My situation is different. I have circumstances I cannot control. My circumstances are harder. My story is different."

We *all* have circumstances we cannot control. We *all* have obstacles in our path we didn't put there. We don't have control of the situation we were born into. We don't have control of our families or the people around us.

Luckily, we always have control of what *we do*. We do have control of our next steps.

TEN YEAR OLD SHATTERED

When my husband was ten he was out playing basketball with his friends. It was a perfectly carefree January. He was warm, happy, and full of possibility. Across town, his parents were rear ended by another vehicle as they were making a left turn.

Neither of them survived.

In the time it took this ten-year-old kid to play a game of basketball both his parents were dead.

One minute he was just like every other kid, the next he was desperately alone. The thing about losing both of your parents is that you lose your entire world. You don't just lose the people you loved more than anything in the world, you lose everything.

He didn't have a home anymore. He didn't know where he was going to sleep that night, who was going to feed him, how he would get to school, or how to get clean clothes.

He lost everything.

For the next four years of his life he would bounce around from house to house trying to find a new place to call home. Sometimes he was with one of his sisters, sometimes he was alone.

In seconds, this kid's life was torn apart.

There was nothing he could do about his parents' death or the people who were willing to take him in. This is a circumstance he had absolutely no control over. There was nothing he could do.

> Nobody would have blamed him if he had completely fallen apart.

Everyone would have understood if he quit playing sports, let his grades drop, and stopped contributing to his life. Nobody would have blamed him if he had turned to self medication in his teenage years. Everyone would have looked at him with pity saying things like, "He had a really hard road. It was the best he could do."

That isn't what my husband chose to do.

He stepped up. He learned how to take care of himself. He chose to keep moving forward. He made good friends, he made good life choices, he kept his wits about him, he chose to put one foot in front of the other and keep moving forward. He was an excellent student. He graduated from college with honors.

Yes, it was hard. Yes, he had really, really bad days. Yes, he was angry. But he kept moving forward.

(p.s. He had a really amazing aunt and uncle who took him in about four years after his parents death. But that is a story for another time.)

A RESTAURANT OF HIS OWN

I met a couple at a business conference several months ago, as they told me their story, my jaw hit the floor. They were both latino and their native language was Spanish.

After five years of Spanish classes I can say three things: "Hola! Me llamo es Dora." "Donde es baño?" and all of the lyrics to *Genie in a Bottle*. (I am only kind of kidding, I only know half the lyrics to *Genie in a Bottle*.)

Luckily, this couple was better versed in English than I was in Spanish.

Throughout lunch, I learned the husband of the couple had come from Peru to the US. It was a harrowing story ending in him arriving in the US with only $100 to his name. $100. He didn't speak the language. He didn't have a place to live. He didn't know anyone.

He could have chosen to do a lot of things. He chose to take a menial job at a restaurant. There he learned everything he could about running a restaurant. He threw himself into learning, asking questions, and figuring things out.

A few years later he opened his own restaurant serving food from his home country. He didn't just open a restaurant. He opened a place that provides for his family. A business that made it through COVID. A business he is looking to expand in the next year.

He opened his own restaurant.

This man chose to do more with his life. He chose to step up and step out of his own way. He chose to create the life he left his country for.

MENTAL HEALTH ISSUES SAY WHAT?

I am dyslexic. Yes, I am dyslexic and I wrote a book. ^I will hold for applause.^ It didn't come easily. A lot of people had to read this to find all my typos and mixed up words, but ... I did it. I have combined ADHD. I have a sensory disorder, clinical anxiety, and insomnia. I also have one doctor who keeps telling me I am bi-polar but I don't like that diagnosis so I am ignoring it.

I have three kids. I grew up in, and am still part of, a religion that generally likes women to be homemakers. I live in a tiny community who often supports the rhetoric that I should be at home. I live in a rural area with one, single stop light. It took us ten years longer than anyone else to get the internet! We lose power when the wind blows.

I didn't graduate from college. My dad was a police officer. We were not wealthy.

And, I have built six businesses from the ground up. I have sold four businesses. I have been published in national magazines. I have national customer service awards. I support my family with my business. I wrote a book. I have clients all over the world, coast to coast and in multiple countries.

I bring up these stories not to brag or make anyone's obstacles seem more or less important. I bring them up because everyone has *something*. We have a circumstance (or fifteen) in our lives that makes things hard. We have situations we can't control. These situations can feel debilitating. You are not alone. You are not the only person going through hard crap.

I am here to tell you you don't have to take what you are handed.

We all have privilege. We all have something that someone else yearns for. What good are these privileges and blessings if we are not using them to better our lives and the lives of those around us?

You have things that someone else is jealous of. Be grateful for those things. Use them to become more than you are right now.

I genuinely believe we control our future, especially for anyone living in the US where we do have significantly fewer restrictions than many other countries. You can do hard things. *You can.*

> One of the biggest issues we face is getting out of our own way and letting ourselves take the risks to keep chipping away at our goals when we are terrified.

HOW TO KEEP MOVING FORWARD

My husband took me hiking straight up a cliff once, all so we could stand under a giant arch and take a picture. I was 100% sure I was going to die.

I am not a hiker. I am a scaredy-cat. Along our hike we had to stop several times for me to build up my courage and catch my breath. My husband babied me along our hike while I literally crawled my way up this cliff trying not to quit. Or cry. ^I am quite a skilled hiker.^

Business ownership is intense. Sometimes we need to stop to catch our breath. We need to gather our courage before we can move again. Being a business owner does automatically endow you with courage. Courage is not something you wake up one day and just have. Courage is built one rest stop at a time, day by day, little by little.

Courage is built in the moments we decide to go on instead of turn back.

But how do we bring ourselves to keep going when sometimes turning back seems so much easier? Here are three tools that keep me on my feet when I am not sure I can make it.

TOOL ONE: LOOKING BACK

Hiking up that monstrous cliff, looking up at our destination felt exhausting.

No matter how many steps I took I still felt like I wasn't an inch to the top. The ridiculous arch was never any closer. I walked and wheezed and trudged but I swear that stupid arch was never any closer.

In contrast, every time I stopped, sat, and looked back down the cliff I was surprised I had come so far.

That stupid arch (that you could see perfectly well from the road) never seemed any closer - the journey seemed just as hard and long halfway up as it did at the bottom.

When I looked back, I realized I was making significantly more progress than I thought. I used that progress to help propel me forward.

Sometimes, in business,

> we are so determined to get where we want to go we forget to draw strength from where we came from.

When was the last time you really looked back at the progress you have made so far? Where were you a year ago? What about five years ago?

It's important to keep track of our achievements. When we know what we have accomplished, we are more prepared for the hard moments. When we reach a hard and scary moment we are equipped to stop, sit, and look where we are, what tools we have, and what we have done. We can draw strength from what we have accomplished.

Look at where you are and where you came from. What are some of the things you have accomplished? Is there anything you are incredibly proud of? What have you done that you never gave yourself credit for?

I recently did this exercise with the women in my Launch Your Business Academy. I set the timer, I made them write for five minutes. They were not overly excited when we started. When we finished they were *glowing*.

We are not aware of how far we have come in life. How far we have come in a year. We cross tasks off each day only to move onto the next one. Those little tasks add up. Those little tasks can completely change your life in the course of a year.

What do you have now you didn't have when you started? What have you already accomplished?

TOOL TWO: WORST CASE

The next tool to help you keep going is called the worst case scenario. In my hiking story, I thought I could actually die. I was sure death was imminent.

When I have babies, I get some pretty fantastic pre and postpartum depression. Right before my last baby was born I was with my therapist, absolutely reeling about my life disaster. I didn't know what my family was going to do. I lost all of my contracts during COVID. I was mentally a huge mess and I couldn't figure out how to rebound or pivot. I felt like everything was falling apart.

I genuinely could not think of a way out.

My therapist asked what the worst case scenario was, if the absolutely worst happened, what would it be? I was ready. I had months of anxiety to prepare for this question. I was going to lose my house, my savings, I would be homeless, have my kids taken away, and die in a van on the side of the highway.

I expected her to be really concerned, to panic, to spiral with me. Clearly this was a catastrophe! Instead she asked me a simple question, "What things will you do before you let that happen?"

I was confused. I wasn't prepared for solutions. I wasn't even sure I understood the question. So she asked again,"If you can't get the contracts. If you close your business, what steps will you take before you lose your house?"

Clearly, she hadn't been listening.

> There were no options. Everything was ruined. We
> had no money, no income, no prospects.

She just looked at me.

Very, very slowly I processed, finally saying, "I guess my husband could go back to work." Another long pause, "I can get a 9-5." Another pause, "And we have savings we can use."

My husband could get a real job. That was the real worst case scenario. My husband could go back to work. How had I never realized that?

In the end, my situation wasn't nearly as dire as I had thought. The worst case scenario wasn't dying in a van, it was my husband going back to work. That's not bad. For most couples that's normal.

We do this a lot. We create worst case scenarios that are crazy extreme things we would never let happen.

When you start to spiral, take a minute. Take a minute and ask yourself what steps you will take before you let that worst case scenario happen. What can you do to prevent complete and total collapse?

In my rock climbing journey, my worst case was I would fall, die, and/or break all of my bones. ^I was certainly going to be paralyzed for life^. What was I doing to prevent this from happening? Well, my husband was behind me and he was using his hands to make footholds for me whenever I needed them. It also wasn't really a cliff as much as a slightly steep hill.

I was being careful about where I walked. I was taking breaks. I had someone to catch me. A fall would be more like a scary roll. In reality, death was highly unlikely.

Also, children hiked this path all the time... The situation wasn't near as bad as it felt to me.

Sometimes when we ask ourselves what the worst case scenario is we have an incredible un-dramatic answer.

Years ago, I was at a business retreat, learning about sales from my mentor and my business coach. They wanted me to make sales calls.

I wanted to crawl into a hole and never come out again. I felt sick to my stomach.

While I was fumbling through my excuses my mentor interrupted me, "So, what is the worst that can happen?" I stopped, thought and thought and said, "Well, I guess they can say no and hang up on me. Or yell."

"Okay," she said, "They probably will. How will that change your whole life?"

Well obviously, it wouldn't change my whole life. It felt dramatic and terrifying but, in the end, someone saying no is not a big deal at all. I just went to the next name on my list and started again.

(And by the way, during that day of pushing through fear and selling anyway I had 30 acres of land donated to me for the project I was working on.)

TOOL THREE: MAKE A PLAN

Tool number three is to make a plan. Sometimes we stand at the top of a cliff thinking, "If I jump off this thing I will probably die." That is a legitimate concern. If you jump off a cliff your chances of survival are not great. I do not recommend jumping off cliffs.

You can walk away, jump anyway and hope you survive, or you can come up with a way to make it down the cliff.

You can get the proper training and gear to make it down, you can find an alternate route, you can parasail, you can sled, you can roll, you can go around. There are options to getting down your big cliff.

The same is true in business. We have metaphorical cliffs we need to climb or get down. We can stare at them all day and hope they go away. Sometimes we stare at them for years. Or we can make a plan, figure out how to tackle these problems, and move forward. We can find support, coaching, education, programs, mentors, loans, etc. etc.

If you don't know where to start, the Launched communities on Facebook are a great place to find support and start brainstorming the next plans in your business. You don't have to be stuck.

Brainstorm and start creating a plan.

FEAR IS PART OF LIFE

There is nothing wrong with getting stuck. There is nothing wrong with feeling afraid.Fear is part of life. The issue comes when we let fear or feelings of discouragement keep us from moving forward. If we let the distance of that arch keep us from moving, we will never reach our goals. We want to develop the tools to function within the fear. We want to know how to keep moving when things get hard.

If you made it to the end of this book you have a lot of tools. Now you just need to make sure you keep going.

NEURAL PATHWAYS

Doing scary things gets easier. Every time we give ourselves permission to screw up it eases our mental pressure and actually helps us make fewer mistakes.

> If we have been running from fear for a long time,
> we have mental wiring telling us running away is the
> correct response to fear.

It can feel like an instinct. It can feel almost impossible to do anything but run.

There are pathways in our brains to help make choices easier. These are called neural pathways. Each time we make a choice in life (like choosing to run away vs stay and face our fear), our brain creates a kind of pathway. When the same choice is made over and over again that pathway becomes more well-worn, an easy road to travel.

For instance, my patience pathway is like a little, tiny game trail. While my "procrastinate until it goes away" pathway is basically a super highway.

Every day we have forks in our mental pathways. We can choose to be angry, happy, sad, or anything in between. Each time we make a choice our brain is more likely to lean towards the same choice the next time and the next time.

In my life, I have usually chosen anger.

I had programmed my brain to go to anger first. It was almost an instinct. For a long time I didn't really have an anger pathway anymore. It was more like a full-on highway. I was often halfway down that highway before I even realized I made the choice to take it.

I cultivated this anger highway. One side was lined with all the lies I had told myself. These were quotes and saying that I posted on metaphorical billboards down my highway. I used these to justify my behavior, the reasons it is okay to be angry, to yell, and to tell losers they were stupid. They said things like, "If I won't, who will?" "Sometimes you have to get angry to get things done." and "If you aren't part of the solution, you are part of the problem."

The other side of the highway was lined with all the people that ^supported^ me. I say supported sarcastically because these people didn't really support me, they just stood behind my aggressiveness saying, "good job" so they didn't have to do it themselves.

I know, I have been one of them.

Each quote on my highway wasn't bad. The people "cheering" me on weren't bad. But I was using them to justify my anger, the way it made me feel, and the

251

way I was treating others.

I had played into my anger, I fed it. I told anger it was right until my brain believed that was the correct response.

Then I believed it.

Choosing a different path was not easy for me. My new pathway was not a well-maintained highway, it was a small and bumpy trail that probably had a cliff on one side because that scares me.

But the more I chose this pathway, the easier it became to choose it again and again.

My tiny trail became a well-maintained path. I hope, eventually it will become its own highway. It can become the choice my brain starts to make automatically.

Choosing to step into your fear is hard.

It will feel like you are on this teeny, tiny, path down a mountainside. Your soul will want to be on the big, safe, well lit highway. It gets better. The more you make the choice to be brave, the easier bravery becomes.

I had a mentor/colleague for just a little while but he was great. He was the first person who taught me this concept. He told me if I am pushing myself the right way, I will start to crave the scared feeling in my gut. He told me he knows he isn't doing his best if he doesn't feel "the fear."

^He sounded like a masochist to me.^

I laughed off his weird advice, he was obviously just trying to push me to do the thing he wanted me to do.

Year later, I get it.

I have learned to manage that fear in my gut. And you know what, it isn't so scary anymore. It means I am trying, it means I am extending myself, it means

I am reaching a new level. He was right. I look for it. I look for it to know if I am playing it safely or if I am taking big action towards my goals.

Take big action.

DREAMS ARE SAFEST WHEN THEY ARE DREAMS

We like to keep our dreams as dreams because they are safer that way.

If we take the steps to actually accomplishing our dreams we risk losing them. We risk failing and that is insanely scary.

But what is the other option?

My senior year of high school I ran for class president. I had two friends running for class offices and they convinced me to run with them. I was terrified. I wasn't terrified of being in charge, or doing the job. I was pretty sure I could do a great job.

I was terrified of losing.

I didn't want to look disappointed if I lost. I didn't want to put my all out there and then be crushed if I couldn't win. I was running against a girl who was much more popular than me. I didn't want to look foolish when no one voted for me.

So, I didn't try.

I did less than the bare minimum. I was running for class president, a secret class president who didn't hang up posters, who didn't tell anyone, who didn't prepare a speech. I simply hoped that people would see my name and maybe vote.

I devastatingly lost that election, of course I did. I never took the steps to win.

I never took the steps to try.

If we choose to never take the steps, if we never chase that dream we are choosing to fail.

> We lose our dream just by a failure to act.

This is your one life. This isn't a dress rehearsal, this is it! You CAN do hard things and it's okay if it makes you nervous.

Michael Jordan didn't make his school basketball team. He could have quit. He could have slid all the way down that hill, never playing again.

He didn't.

JK Rowling is the second highest paid author of all time.

Do you know how many times Harry Potter was rejected? Twelve. Twelve times people told her no, told her her story wasn't good enough.

She didn't scrap everything and start again. She kept going. Are you willing to massively fail that many times in your business?

Be willing. We will all fail. We will all screw up.

> Give yourself permission to not be perfect, then keep moving forward.

You can do hard things. DO the scary things anyway.

I CAN DO HARD THINGS

When my oldest kid was in kindergarten the school made all the kindergartens shirts saying, "I can do hard things." They were adorable and my cute kindergartener wore his all of the time. He was this super, sweet kid who was very intune with my emotions.

He always knew when to crack a joke or when to crawl into my lap and just hug me.

He very quickly became my own personal motivational poster, in t-shirt form. I was doing a lot of really scary things in business that year. I wasn't sure what I was really capable of. I was scared a lot. When I was trying to be brave he would run to his room, change his clothes, and come back in that "I can do hard things" shirt, just for me. "You can do hard things, mom."

You can do hard things.

It is silly how much that phrase has become an almost daily mantra for me. I had a friend this week tell my husband he doesn't worry about me when bad things happen because he knows I will figure it out.

He is right, I will figure it out -- but not because I have a magic pill. I am just as flawed and broken and tired as everyone else.

I "figure it out" because I am constantly telling myself I can do hard things.

> Even when I want to crawl in a hole and live there,
> there is a little part of me saying, "You can do
> hard things".

I see that little five-year-old in my head telling me the same thing. "You can do hard things, Mom."

Whatever you are dealing with, whatever is making you want to crawl in a hole, just know you can do hard things.

You can do hard things.

Go out there and make your dreams happen. No one can do it but you.

I know you can figure it out. You can do hard things.

NEXT STEPS

Stop dreaming.

Get moving.

Life will not stop and wait for you.

Scan the code or visit:
launchedacademy.com/book-bonuses

WORK CITED

A., Julija, and Small Biz Genius. "40+ Small Business Statistics: The Ultimate 2023 List." *SmallBizGenius,* June 2023, https://www. smallbizgenius.net/by-the-numbers/small-business-statistics/. Accessed 31 July 2023.

Alaimo, Dan. "87% of shoppers now begin product searches online." *Retail Dive,* 15 August 2018, https://www.retaildive.com/news/87-of-shoppers-now-begin-product-searches-online/530139/. Accessed 31 July 2023.

Bregman, Peter, and Harvard Business Review. "How (and Why) to Stop Multitasking." *Harvard Business Review*, 20 May 2010, https://hbr.org/2010/05/how-and-why-to-stop-multitaski. Accessed 31 July 2023.

Djuraskovic, Ogi. "eCommerce Statistics (2023) - 33 Useful Stats and Facts." *FirstSiteGuide*, 17 April 2023, https://firstsiteguide.com/ecommerce-stats/. Accessed 31 July 2023.

Farris, Paul W. *Marketing Metrics: The Definitive Guide to Measuring Marketing Performance.* FT Press, 2010.

Hotjar. "Ecommerce: 23 Insightful Stats on Shopping Cart Abandonment." *Hotjar*, 2 January 2023, https://www.hotjar.com/blog/cart-abandonment-stats/. Accessed 31 July 2023.

Howarth, Josh. "22+ Referral Marketing Statistics (New For 2023)." *Exploding Topics*, 25 April 2023, https://explodingtopics.com/blog/referral-marketing-stats. Accessed 31 July 2023.

Jawed, Soyiba, et al. "Classification of Visual and Non-visual Learners Using Electroencephalographic Alpha Gamma Activities." *Frontiers in Behavioral Neuroscience*, vol. 13, no. 86, 2019, . *National Library of*

Medicine, https://doi.org/10.3389/fnbeh.2019.00086. Accessed 31 July 2023.

Mark, Gloria, et al. "The Cost of Interrupted Work: More Speed and Stress." *Proceedings of ACM CHI 2008 Conference of Human Factors in Computing Systems*, Interaction Design Foundation, 2008, pp. 107-110. https://doi.acm.org/10.1145/1357054.1357072, https://www.ics.uci.edu/~gmark/chi08-mark.pdf.

Naghdi, Arash, and Dream Farm Studios. "How does shape language impact character design?" *Dream Farm Studios*, 6 April 2023, https://dreamfarmstudios.com/blog/shape-language-in-character-design/. Accessed 31 July 2023.

Newland, Stephen. "The Power of Accountability." *AFCPE*, 2018, https://www.afcpe.org/news-and-publications/the-standard/2018-3/the-power-of-accountability/. Accessed 31 July 2023.

Pokora, Becky, and Toni Perkins. "Credit Card Statistics And Trends 2023 – Forbes Advisor." *Forbes*, 9 March 2023, https://www.forbes.com/advisor/credit-cards/credit-card-statistics/. Accessed 31 July 2023.

Reed, Betsy. "Women are happier without children or a spouse, says happiness expert." *The Guardian*, 25 May 2019, https://www.theguardian.com/lifeandstyle/2019/may/25/women-happier-without-children-or-a-spouse-happiness-expert. Accessed 31 July 2023.

Rioux, Patricia, and Forbes. "The Value of Investing in Loyal Customers." *Forbes*, 29 June 2020, https://www.forbes.com/sites/forbesagencycouncil/2020/01/29/the-value-of-investing-in-loyal-customers/?sh=15ec976221f6. Accessed 31 July 2023.

Sekulic, Radovan. "How Many People Use PayPal in 2023?" *Moneyzine*, 27 February 2023, https://moneyzine.com/personal-finance-resources/how-many-people-use-paypal/. Accessed 31 July 2023.

Walt Disney Family Museum. "Shape Language: Tips and Techniques." *Walt Disney Family Museum*, 04 2020, https://www.waltdisney.org/sites/default/files/2020-04/T%26T_ShapeLang_v9.pdf. Accessed 31 July 2023.

Wood, Meredith. "What Is the Average Small Business Owner Salary in the U.S.?" *Fundera*, 11 November 2020, https://www.fundera.com/blog/study-finds-business-owners-earn-less. Accessed 31 July 2023.

Zimmerman, Eilene, and Forbes. ".,:;"-' Only 2% Of Women-Owned Businesses Break The $1 Million Mark -- Here's How To Be One Of Them." .,:;"-' - *Forbes*, 22 June 2023, https://www.forbes.com/sites/eilenezimmerman/2015/04/01/only-2-of-women-owned-businesses-break-the-1-million-mark-heres-how-to-be-one-of-them/?sh=218bdcb327a6. Accessed 31 July 2023.